My Unknown Soldier

A History of the 4th Massachusetts
Infantry Regiment in the Civil War

By
Nancy O. Weber

BURD STREET PRESS
SHIPPENSBURG, PENNSYLVANIA

This Burd Street Press publication
was printed by
Beidel Printing House, Inc.
63 West Burd Street
Shippensburg, PA 17257-0708 USA

The acid-free paper used in this book meets the guidelines for permanence and durability of the Committee on Production Guidelines for Book Longevity of the Council on Library Resources.

For a complete list of available publications
please write
Burd Street Press
Division of White Mane Publishing Company, Inc.
P.O. Box 708
Shippensburg, PA 17257-0708 USA

Library of Congress Cataloging-in-Publication Data

Weber, Nancy O., 1935-
    My unkown soldier : a history of the 4th Massachusetts Infantry Regiment in the Civil War / by Nancy O. Weber
        p. cm.
    Transcription of diary of soldier, most likely John Dennis: with supplemental material on the regiment which saw service in Louisiana.
    Includes bibliographical references and index.
    ISBN 1-57249-296-1 (alk. paper)
    1. United States. Army Massachusetts Infantry Regiment, 4th (1862-1863)--History. 2. United States--History--Civil War, 1861-1865--Personal narratives. 3. Massachusetts--History--Civil War, 1861-1865--Personal narratives. 4. Louisiana--History--Civil War, 1861-1865--Personal narratives. 5. Soldiers--Massachusetts--Diaries. I. Dennis, John, d. 1911. II. Title.

E513.5 4th .W43 2002
973.7'444--dc21

                                                                    2001058108

That victory at Manassas did nothing but send us off in a fool's paradise of conceit and it roused the manhood of the Northern people.

—Mary Chestnut, *A Diary from Dixie*

Contents

Illustrations and Maps

Foreword

This book has been a compelling force in my life since the day six years ago when a generous woman placed a weather-beaten, battle-scarred Civil War diary in my hand. It was devoid of the author's name and that was even more incentive for me to determine its owner and tell his story.

I am not an historian by education but have been a Civil War history addict for years. I approached this challenge by methodically examining this phase of the war wherever the diary took me. The greatest mystery was determining who was the author of the diary. That compulsion directed me to archives, libraries, museums, the United States Army Military Institute, and some very meaningful research time in Massachusetts. In Lawrence, Massachusetts, the Lawrence Public Library and Immigrant City Archives provided my first positive lead to the diary's author. The North Andover Court House and Historical Society helped me to confirm some facts and supplied information that filled in several blanks. There were false assumptions, misdirections, and frustrations in determining the author of the diary. Eventually, the list of possible identities contained the name of one man whom I believe to be the diary's author. Because research does not always provide that final piece of information necessary to make a proof-positive statement, I have titled this book, *My Unknown Soldier*. I am sure I know his name, but after one hundred thirty-plus years, time has erased the unequivocal proof.

This is the story of the relatively unknown 4th Massachusetts Infantry Regiment, a nine-month unit that served in

Louisiana. A list of all their names, by company, is included in the appendix of this book. It is my hope that the reader will gain insight to the cruel reality, boredom, and hardships that these men endured. Theirs is a story that has not yet been formally told.

Acknowledgments

My sincere appreciation to my family and friends who listened patiently as I shared my experiences with them over the life of this research. Special thanks to my daughters and sons-in-law, Nancy and Phil Harris and Sue and Sean McGee, who previewed my manuscript and listened to my reasons why something should remain even if they disagreed. I will forever be indebted to my dear friend, Helen Turner, who spent hours reviewing the manuscript drafts, offering excellent editorial advice, and urging me on when the words, facts, and manuscript composition became a huge blur. Thank you, too, to my husband, Ron Weber, who I dragged through historical societies, museums, and ancient cemeteries.

There are also other people to whom I owe a great deal and without whom this book would never have been written. They include:

Paul Bucher, Professional Historian Researcher. Thank you for the many hours spent chasing my numerous requests and questions.

Frances Griffin. Mrs. Griffin, you are not only a dear friend but also provided the diary that piqued my interest, inspired my research, and initiated this book.

Robert Hull. Although our only contacts were by letter and telephone, you generously offered your time and ingenuity in helping me track down the author of the diary.

Ronald J. Simeone, Examiner of Questioned Documents. Your expertise in the analysis of handwriting kept me honest and avoided assumptions not based on fact.

Ken Skulski, Professional Researcher. Your enthusiasm and interest in history are so contagious that it made sifting through old records a fun experience.

Introduction

From There to Here

I have always been amazed how possessions get from "there,"(i.e., the location where they were used, stored, or purchased) to "here," often hundreds to thousands of miles away from their origin. The "here" (where the item finally comes to rest) may be an antique shop, a private home, a subject-specific retail show, an estate sale, or any number of ordinary places. Whenever I buy historical items, I question the sellers for background information. They usually do not know the source of the items or, at the very best, there are vague references to a state or general locality. This book owes its existence to a diary that represents the "there to here" anomaly.

The diary came purely by chance into my possession. On one of my many trips to the mountains of Virginia, I had the good fortune to meet a woman well versed in local history. She is able to pinpoint all of the places mentioned in Civil War historic books despite the fact that names have been changed over the years, or locations are only vaguely described. We became very good friends, spending hours touring back roads and finding forgotten cemeteries and home sites. One day she gave me the diary, which would consume my life for six years.

The physical appearance of the diary is most unimpressive—torn, dirty, and without the front and back cover and thus no author's name. It is very small, measuring about three by four inches, a typical old pocket ledger. It is written in brown ink and pencil, which has faded over the last one hundred thirty-plus years, but the contents are priceless to any Civil

War enthusiast. It was written by a Union soldier, who saw family separation, war, and death, but returned home despite the odds. The from "there to here" drama played out when I asked about the diary's origins. The owner knew only that it was in the top drawer of a chest that she had purchased at an antique shop in Pennsylvania many years earlier.

This diary is a record kept by a foot soldier for either his own edification or as a record for his wife and children. I believe the author was an unusual man, who cared enough to write his experiences, some in detail. Perhaps he was a methodical type, who liked to keep records, or maybe this was an adventure he needed to record for later recall. Whatever his motivation, he documented a significant piece of history. There are many Civil War diaries that contain more information and personal interpretation. Those types of records have provided numerous historical facts and individual revelations that would have been lost in the "cut and dried" field and battle reports. I look with envy upon such epistles, but this diary is not one of them. The daily entries are short with gaps in time; some of his notes cry out for elaboration. If only he had mentioned another name or filled in another day's activities. Yet, we do know that it is a record of a very obscure military unit in an obscure military engagement during the Civil War. Additionally, it is his own unedited, first-hand account of his wartime experiences.

Transcribing the diary was a long, tedious process. I could only work for a limited period of time under strong light using a magnifying glass. My first assumption was that the diary had been written by a soldier from Pennsylvania, after all that is where it was found. Then I read aloud the first five pages, and I could decipher an accent. "Has" is written as "as"; "had" is written as "ad." Everything is spelled phonetically, and he certainly drops his "h's." It definitely appears to be similar to a New England accent. The author of the diary seems to have had minimal education, but his handwriting is legible, and his capital letters are in the beautiful script taught in schools well over a hundred years ago. Further into the diary, he mentions his wife but never records her name. I later discovered that the diarist played a horn in the military band, and enjoyed his whiskey. Pages later he states, "Since we left Massctusts..." so I do know New England was home, but where and what unit did he serve in? More details evolve as entries list the names of several men from his company who were wounded in an attack on a ship in the New Orleans area. Research reveals that these men were all from Company B, 4th Massachusetts Infantry Regiment. I had identified the unit but had yet to discover the writer's name.

The 4th Massachusetts Infantry Regiment was recruited for nine months of military service serving in 1862 and 1863. They were sent to Louisiana and participated in the battle of Port Hudson on the Mississippi River. Very few books have been written about the Port Hudson campaign, and those that have been written usually make reference to the fact that, historically, the battle has been neglected. This is most likely because the Port Hudson action occurred at the same time that General Grant was in front of Vicksburg, Mississippi. Grant's campaign was much larger in terms of manpower and, thus, is well documented.

Records of the 4th Massachusetts Infantry and books written about the unit are nonexistent. The history of the entire unit seems to have fallen into obscurity. There are no muster rolls, pay records, or enlistment papers available. All company records and a great deal of the company's personal belongings were captured and destroyed by the Confederates in Brashear City, Louisiana, on June 23, 1863. Essentially the only tracking mechanisms that remain are official reports, state rosters, and pension records.

By pure luck and an obscure footnote, I did locate another diary written by a 4th Massachusetts Infantry soldier. This diary was written by Corporal James F. Dargan, Company D, who enlisted at the age of 19. His account has helped in filling in the gaps that exist in my diary and will be referenced occasionally in this book. Corporal Dargan paid great attention to detail, although his diary exists as an edited version and was completed approximately 10 years after the war. Dargan's records provide another example of the from "there to here" paradox. The diary is held in the special collection of the California State University Library, Northridge, California, and, according to the library staff, was purchased years ago from a dealer in Civil War antiquities. It is doubtful that Dargan, a Massachusetts native, ever lived in California. He died in Buffalo, New York, in 1882.

Additionally, I managed to locate a book written by Captain Henry B. Maglathlin, Company I, 4th Massachusetts Infantry. It contains a roster of Company I and a very brief summary of war events in Louisiana. This book lends further support to the "there to here" paradox since the only copy I have been able to locate is available on interlibrary loan from Rice University in Houston, Texas.

Company B was composed of approximately one hundred three men, 34 of whom were born in England, Scotland, or Ireland. Most were employed by the textile mills in Lawrence, Massachusetts. The only way to determine the diary's author was through a laborious process of elimination. None of the men who were captured at Brashear City in 1863 could have been the diarist, since the diary indicates that the author was not there and heard about the action after it had occurred. I knew the diarist played in a band, so I determined who the musicians were. Two men were designated as band members but were too young to be married, and one had been taken prisoner at Brashear City. A third member of the unit was a music teacher by profession, but again, he would have been too young and did not marry until he returned to Massachusetts in 1863. So, the "military band" lead was dead, at least for the time being.

All commissioned officers could be eliminated since it is obvious from the diary that the author was not in command, rather he was a foot soldier participating in the campaign. Some men were negated purely for their ages since they would have to have been older than their teens in order to be married. Since the author never mentions his wife's name and provides no indication that he thinks about and misses her, it is safe to assume that he had been married for some time. Anyone who was wounded or died before the unit's return to Massachusetts was eliminated. This process left more than 40 men as possibilities.

When the diary provides details, they are accurate. The author lists men's names, all correct when checked against company rolls, and he lists almost exactly the armament and number of prisoners captured at Port Hudson. Such detail indicates that he may have been a noncommissioned officer, perhaps an orderly sergeant or corporal in charge of company records and reports. There were four noncommissioned officers who qualified; research of pension records reduced that number to one.

The one qualifying noncommissioned officer was Aaron A. Currier, 25 years old, a carpenter from Lawrence, Massachusetts, and a sergeant in Company B, 4th Massachusetts Infantry Regiment. He could have been the orderly sergeant and, as such, would have had access to all the information contained in the diary. In addition, Currier's records from the National Archives and Records Administration indicate that he was on detached duty for a period of time with the captain of the company. This detail meant he was not at Brashear City, but could have been involved in the Fort

Bisland and Port Hudson, Louisiana, encounters described in the diary.

Conclusive proof could only be obtained by comparing the handwriting contained in the diary with subsequent documents written by Sergeant Currier. Pension records provide a later sample of handwriting, but are dated to almost 40 years after the diary had been written. I have been unable to locate anything written by Currier during that 40-year gap with the exception of one signature dated 1867. Currier had been very active in the Masons, and his obituary listed his lodge associations. A gentleman who has conducted a significant amount of research on Masonic history in Lawrence provided me with Currier's signature, taken from old meeting records. The professional document examiner who reviewed the diary and subsequent signatures concluded that Sergeant Currier could not have been the author of the diary. The handwriting just did not match. By this point, I knew so much about Sergeant Currier personally that I was disappointed to find out he was not the author. My research friends in Lawrence also experienced the same letdown.

In the process of reviewing historical material in Lawrence, I did discover the city roll book, a document maintained by each locality in the state of Massachusetts. It was mandated by law and was used as a record of bounty payments made by the town, city, or county. Evidently, upon the end of the enlistment period and the regiment's return to Massachusetts, a city clerk made appropriate entries after each soldier's name if they had deviated from the conditions of their enlistment. These notations did not include changes in rank, but rather assignment changes and any fact that may have affected the payment of the bounty.

The Lawrence roll book contains several notations that were made after Company B returned in 1863. A remark was placed after each soldier's name indicating whether he had been involved in the mutiny at Port Hudson. It was an unfortunate situation that occurred more than one hundred thirty years ago, and their identities here would not serve a meaningful purpose. I found no indication that these men were denied payment of their bounties. There are, however, two notations that enabled me to identify the authorship of the diary. Musicians were instructed as soldiers and were required to serve in the ranks. Upon enlistment, a man was initially designated as "musician" based upon his talent for music. That was an important differentiation since musicians received an additional stipend above the normal soldier's salary. A notation in the Lawrence roll book indicated that one of the men, who enlisted as a musician, was incompetent, or essentially, he had no talent for music. He would have had to have been replaced and, according to the roll book, he was by a man whose name shows the insertion of the notation "rank musician." The diary's author played in the band on several occasions, so he must have been considered to be competent.

The "rank musician" was John Dennis, approximately 32 years old and born in England in about 1830. He worked in the textile mills in Lawrence either as a spinner or a machinist and was married with three children by the fall of 1862. There were several bands in Lawrence during that time frame but, unfortunately, records no longer exist identifying the members by name. The accent that I detected while transcribing the diary had not necessarily been that of a New Englander, but of a man born in England. Dennis died in 1911 after suffering for years from chronic dysentery, an ailment mentioned in the diary. A minibiography of Private Dennis is included in the appendix.

As in the case of Sergeant Currier, a comparison of handwriting was necessary for unequivocal proof. The pension records of Private Dennis provide signatures spanning the years from 1864 to 1907, but no paper trail from him exists to compare with the diary's handwriting. The spacing of letters and strokes as compared to the diary and later signatures are very similar. The professional document examiner's final decision on Private Dennis is that it is probable, but not conclusive, that he wrote the diary. A totally conclusive identification could only be reached if I could locate something other than a signature written by Private Dennis after 1863.

I am reasonably certain of the identity of the diarist, but have not proven it without a shadow of a doubt. There is still the missing piece of handwriting an expert needs to declare that Private Dennis is the writer of the diary. This in no way lessens my desire to tell the story of Currier, Dennis, and their fellow members of the 4th Massachusetts Infantry Regiment before time obliterates its history.

Included in the text are all the entries from the diary recorded as the author had written them. His phonetic spelling, in most cases, is not difficult to decipher. I have included in brackets the correct spelling when in question. I have added all of the "h's" to his "has" and "had's" for easier reading. Although this book is primarily about the soldiers from Lawrence who joined the 4th Massachusetts Infantry, it is essentially the history of the entire regiment as it disembarked from home, fought in Louisiana, and returned to Massachusetts.

Chapter I

The Fall of 1862
Call to Arms

The Civil War officially began when Fort Sumter surrendered to the Confederate forces on April 14, 1861. One day later, President Abraham Lincoln called for 75,000 men to enter the Federal army for 90 days in a war he called an "insurrection." Patriotism was on fire, and some Northern states declared that they would exceed quotas. The states promised that the president would have more soldiers than he could handle.

The secessionist states struggled with their new government, but they too saw this as a "short war" and mustered militia to protect states' rights. Maryland and the border states of Kentucky, Tennessee, and Missouri were torn apart by individual loyalties. Even Virginia did not present a united front. The northwestern part of the state had no interest in states' rights, after all they were mountain men, not plantation owners and business men. Life was hard enough without being involved in some political struggle.

Historians tell us the fortunes of war are in the hands of a few, and the population follows where leaders are the strongest. The Civil War was no exception. Two economies were at odds, neither really understood the other, and political factions were hard at work to promote personal causes.

One can only imagine how difficult it was to choose sides. Families were divided, military schoolmates were at opposite ends of the pole, and the entire structure of the United States Army was in chaos. Cool heads warned that this was not a short-term uprising, and hot heads persuaded the country that the only way to settle a long, simmering battle over Federal jurisdiction was war. The Peace Democrats, referred to more popularly as the Copperheads, promoted antiwar feelings, and the abolitionists called for accelerated war efforts.[1]

The fall of 1862 found the country involved in a war almost 18 months old. It had become far more than an insurrection, and the populace reluctantly accepted the reality that it would last even longer. Things were not going well for either side, but the Confederacy was the most threatened. The loss of shipping ports and Northern goods was taking its toll on the Southern economy. The Confederate States of America found themselves in the impossible position of trying to maintain a field army without adequate supplies. There were second thoughts in Washington, too, since maintaining an army rapidly drains an economy. By the end of 1862, the North was spending an astonishing $1.3 million daily to support the war effort, and in 1863, this figure increased to over $2.5 million. The total cost of the Civil War for the Federal government is estimated at over $3 billion.[2]

People in both the North and South were familiar with battles and sites such as Harpers Ferry, Rich Mountain, Bull Run, Fort Donelson, Shiloh, and Antietam. They were also learning the names of men who were controlling military strategy. Almost everyone could talk about and give an opinion of men such as George McClellan, Stonewall Jackson, Robert E. Lee, John Pope, Irvin McDowell, and Ambrose Burnside. President Lincoln knew many of these men very well since he was not only struggling to develop a satisfactory high command, but was also facing strong Confederate opposition.

Thousands of men on both sides had been wounded or killed. The second battle of Bull Run, in August 1862, resulted in over 14,000 casualties for the Federals and over 9,000 for the Confederate army. In the battle of Antietam, 18,440 men were wounded, 4,710 killed, and another 3,043 were missing. All of this carnage at Antietam occurred in approximately 12 hours on September 17, 1862. With such enormous sacrifice, neither side actually won the battle of Antietam nor significantly improved its position in this ongoing war. Lee licked his wounds and slipped back into Virginia while McClellan rested his Federal army and failed to take pursuit.

Disease was an even more wretched killer. Proper sanitary conditions while the soldiers were in camp were ignored, causing men to be exposed to diseases for which they had absolutely no immunity. Measles alone killed thousands of men and had a great deal to do with Lee losing the West Virginia campaign in the fall of 1861. Very few of his men were in any condition to fight, and many men continued to die after his retreat into the lower elevations of Virginia. Disease was not selective of rank, even General McClellan contracted typhoid fever.

It is difficult to believe that there could be any enthusiasm or patriotism left in the country, but there still was, and it was evident on both sides. The Confederacy hoped to force England and France to recognize the Southern cause. The South needed all of the material that the European countries could supply, plus they knew that the North would not risk a war with England if she should side with President Jefferson Davis and his Confederate government. Negotiations for recognition had not been effective thus far, and cotton was the "blackmail" commodity. Plantation production had been cut back, and cotton bales stored at ports such as Charleston and New Orleans were burned by the Confederates when the Federal shipping blockade did not allow the South to ship them to Europe. The foreign markets and Northern textile mills were hurting due to the lack of a cotton supply. Thousands of British mill workers lost their jobs as factories were forced to cut back on production. Russia, who had just entered the textile weaving industry, felt the impact on her economy as the supply of raw material from the Confederate states dwindled to a trickle.[3]

The Mississippi River corridor was the Southern lifeline. Should the Union army control it, the Confederacy would be cut in two. Island No. 10, a Confederate stronghold on the Mississippi River, south of Columbus, Kentucky, fell in April 1862, with the surrender of 3,500 men. On the twenty-fifth of the same month, New Orleans was occupied by the Federal fleet, and June saw the surrender of Memphis, Tennessee, to the Union army. Baton Rouge fell in August even though it was a seesaw affair, and the Union troops moved back to New Orleans three weeks later. Corinth, Mississippi, was captured by the Federals in October 1862, with approximately 2,500 Union men killed, wounded, or missing in action. The army of the Confederacy lost almost twice that number.

By November 1862, Federal troops, with the assistance of naval gunboats on Berwick Bay, had secured the Bayou Lafourche area northwest of New Orleans. This included the settlements of Donaldsonville, Thibodaux, and Brashear City. The Confederacy was still in control of the Mississippi River between Vicksburg, Mississippi, and Port Hudson in southern Louisiana. The Mississippi lifeline and the all-important cotton commodity were in jeopardy. Ironically, at this point in time, the textile mill towns in Massachusetts were recruiting men to join the Union army.

In August 1862, the War Department called for 300,000 more men to serve nine months in the Union army. The nine-month requirement was a reflection of the mind set that the war would end in a short time, plus men were more likely to enlist for a short period rather than to make a three-year commitment. Interestingly, President Lincoln had refused an offer made that same month for two Negro regiments from

Indiana. He was not opposed to using these men as laborers, but the Northern people could not yet comprehend the Negro as a soldier. This point of view would change in a few months, and the men of the 4th Massachusetts Infantry Regiment would fight side by side with the Negro soldier at Port Hudson. The enlistment quota for the state of Massachusetts was 19,080 men. The 4th Massachusetts Infantry Regiment responded although this would not be the first experience for this unit in the Civil War.

The regiment was founded in approximately 1855, when it was called the 4th Regiment, Massachusetts Volunteer Militia, and represented membership from the entire state. In April 1861 the unit responded to the call for troops to settle the "insurrection" in the South, and 635 men enlisted for a three-month period.

The following article appeared in the *Boston Herald* on April 19, 1861, and is indicative of the patriotic sentiments of the era:

> The Fourth Regiment, Col. A. B. Packard, received orders to move at three o'clock on Wednesday, and at four o'clock they presented themselves at the State House exhibiting thereby a commendable promptness, which augurs well for the future. Of their movements until their departure from the city you have been informed, but all along the line of railroad, the rapidly moving train was cheered, and the hearts of the men, who were sacrificing everything for the glorious flag which no true American will ever live to see dishonored, beat high with a hope that the misguided few who have sought to tear in pieces the most glorious fabric of free government which the history of nations records, would soon be compelled to acknowledge the supremacy of the principle that the majority shalt rule.
>
> By eleven o'clock, P.M., all were safely embarked on the Steamer *State of Maine*, and were made as comfortable as circumstances would allow.

The fastenings of the steamer were soon cast off and amid cheering of multitudes and the booming of cannon she shaped her course for New York. The men soon stowed away in their berths, and the night wore on without much interest excepting the huge bonfires which lighted up Newport, disclosing Fort Adams, and indicating the grand flame which has commenced to burn in the hearts of the North, and which will require much conciliation to quench.

A head wind and very rough sea, have caused a very long passage. Fifteen hours already on the boat and not yet in sight of the city. Our five hundred men are, however, in excellent spirits and only impatient to reach the scene of action.

The following commissions have been issued since leaving Boston: Wm. W. Carruth, of Boston, Quartermaster, and a most excellent one too; Wm. D. Atkinson, Jr., of Boston, Paymaster; Franklin Curtis, of Quincy, Capt. Co. H, in place of Newcome, discharged; Luther Stephenson, Jr., of Higham, Capt. Co. F, in place of Sprague, discharged; Edward A. Spear and B. F. Meserve, 1st and 2nd Lieut. Co. H, Quincy, in place of White and Churchill, discharged; Charles Sprague, 3rd Lieut. Co. I, Higham, in place of Burr, discharged. On the staff, Henry Walker of Quincy, Adjutant, in place of H. O. Whittemore, promoted; and Wm. L. Faxon, of Quincy, Surgeon's Mate. In Co. G, Zaccheus Sherman, 2nd Lieut., in place of Sanford, resigned; Frederick A. Harrington, 3rd Lieut., in place of Jas. H. Spear; Wm. R. Black, 4th Lieut., in place of Sherman promoted.

6:10 P.M.—We have reached the metropolis and are now steaming slowly up the East River. Thousands of people line the piers and shipping, and the cheering and salutes of all kinds are continuous and universal. We have come to anchor off the Battery where we shall wait to send and receive dispatches. Capt. Curtis, of Co. H has been detailed as bearer of dispatches to Boston.

Capt. Eldridge of the *State of Maine* is just the man to carry us to our destination, and we hope to remain under his charge if we can.

Certainly a glowing account of men going off to war! There is no question that the citizens of the North were behind Mr. Lincoln. Adjutant Henry Walker, mentioned in the article, returned in 1862, as Colonel Walker, commander of the regiment. The 90-day unit proceeded to Fort Monroe in Virginia, where the 4th Massachusetts mounted guns, dug trenches, and unloaded ships for a month. Fort Monroe was crucial in controlling the strategic waters of Hampton Roads and the first battle of ironclads occurred there in March 1862, between the CSS *Virginia* and the USS *Monitor*.

On May 27, 1861, the 4th Massachusetts moved to Newport News, Virginia, to establish Camp Butler, named after General Benjamin Butler who was in command of the Department of Virginia. Five companies of the 4th Massachusetts took part in the battle of Big Bethel on June 9, 1861, with one man killed and two wounded. In July the unit moved to Hampton, Virginia, and then returned to Boston where the troops were discharged July 22, 1861.

A little more than a year later, the regiment was reformed but very few of the men, who represented the unit in 1861, volunteered again. For the men who came from Lawrence and other Massachusetts towns, enlistment was sweetened by the offer of a $100 bounty paid by their respective town governments. Bounties were also offered by the United States government in the range of $25 to $50. Considering the army pay for a private was $13 a month, these bounties must have been an effective incentive.

September 1862 was the muster-in month for the 4th Massachusetts Infantry Regiment. The field and staff officers were appointed and mustered in sometime during December. Three field officers appointed from Lawrence were Captain Ebenezer Colby, Captain George Merrill, and 1st Lieutenant John Tarbox, all assigned to Company B. These three gentlemen were highly instrumental in recruiting men for their company in Lawrence and certainly were well respected by the men. Albert Dow of Lawrence served as the 2nd lieutenant of Company B.

Captain John Rollins, 1st Lieutenant James Abbott, and 2nd Lieutenant Hiram Robinson, all from Lawrence, were appointed as field officers of Company H. Captain Rollins would find his assignment a difficult one. The men of his company would eventually develop some arbitrary ideas of their own in the Port Hudson campaign.

In total, the 4th Massachusetts Infantry Regiment numbered 980 men. The companies were essentially formed by community representation. It was a good idea for developing an esprit de corps but not when it related to combat losses. Any company involved in a heavy engagement lost men primarily from one town or locality, which was devastating to a community back home. The army would change that practice in subsequent years.

The companies formed in 1862 were as follows:

Company A—101 men primarily from Canton and Stoughton, Massachusetts

Company B—103 men from Lawrence, Massachusetts

Company C—95 men from Middleboro, Massachusetts

Company D—101 men from Randolph, Massachusetts

Company E—94 men primarily from Abington and Bridgewater, Massachusetts

Company F—89 men primarily from Foxboro and Norton, Massachusetts

Company G—95 men from Taunton, Massachusetts

Company H—101 men from Lawrence, Massachusetts

Company I—101 men primarily from Duxbury and Pembroke, Massachusetts

Company J—Was not formed

Company K—100 men from Taunton, Massachusetts[4]

The men of the 4th were no different from the thousands of other raw recruits who entered military service. Army regulations have changed since 1862, but for these Massachusetts men, regulations stipulated that they should bathe once or twice a week, their feet at least twice a week. Hair was to be short and beards well trimmed. The bread they ate was to be well cooked, and the soup was to be boiled at least five hours before being served. The uniform for enlisted men consisted of a dark blue, single-breasted frock coat. Collars and cuffs were edged with a sky-blue cord denoting infantry service. Pants were dark blue with black leather belts, and hats were black felt except for forage caps which were made of a dark blue material with company letters on the front. The shoes were regulation heavy black leather brogans or Jefferson boots. Everyone was to have a tin canteen with a woolen cover, a knapsack, a haversack, and a gray woolen blanket stamped U.S. By fall of 1862, the Union government issued standard equipment including cartridge boxes, U.S. stamped belt plates, and some improved arms.[5]

The 4th Massachusetts Infantry Regiment did have distinctive uniform buttons displaying the number four and were worn by the regiment through the late 1850s but probably not during the Civil War. The button was manufactured by the D. Evans Company in Attleboro, Massachusetts. Most large-button manufacturers were located in New England at that time and utilized the skills and talents of button manufacturers from England. During the Civil War years these manufacturers produced thousands of military buttons for the Union. In addition, they also supplied the Confederacy, via some clandestine ordering procedures. There was money to be made, and many button manufacturers saw no reason to forfeit sales based on Northern loyalty.[6]

A total of 18 men representing the various companies were assigned music designations, leading to the formation of a regimental band. In Company B, one man was designated as an incompetent musician, another deserted from Company C, and in Company K, one man, who was 14 years old, may have been the drummer boy. There does not appear to be any records or photographs of band members in existence with the exception of references made throughout the diary.

On September 12, 1862, the men of Company B, 4th Massachusetts Infantry Regiment, reported to a Federal camp at Wenham, Massachusetts, and were temporarily attached to the 48th Regiment, Massachusetts Volunteers. On December 4, they were ordered to Lakeville, Massachusetts, south of Boston, to continue training as Company B of the 4th Massachusetts Infantry.

Dargan's diary states that his Company D was in Lakeville on September 17, 1862, and spent the following two and one-half months in drill training and general camp duties. There were several furlough periods both for meeting family and serving as an honor guard for the funerals of fellow Massachusetts soldiers who were killed at Antietam. According to his journal, there were many nights when local entertainers visited the camp for a series of plays, concerts, and musicals. The high points were dances attended by the local female population. The usual camp pranks were played, and a number of men utilized "India Rubber" furloughs or, what is called today, unauthorized passes—the AWOLs of the Civil War period.[7]

Chapter II

December 1862–January 1863
Riding the Atlantic

The regiment received training at Camp Joe Hooker in Lakeville, Massachusetts. General Joseph Hooker was born in Massachusetts and graduated from West Point. He had a sterling record as a staff officer in the Mexican War and had resigned from army service in 1853 to become a farmer in California and Oregon. During the early summer of 1862, he was commissioned as a brigadier general of volunteers and soon earned the nickname "Fighting Joe Hooker."

As the troops trained in Lakeville, General Ambrose Burnside was sitting on the Rappahannock River opposite Fredericksburg, Virginia, facing General Lee and the Confederate army. President Lincoln had appointed General Burnside commander of the Army of the Potomac in November 1862, after General McClellan's ineffectiveness at the battle of Antietam.

Much like General McClellan in the past, Burnside hesitated to launch his attack, allowing the Confederate forces time to entrench in the hills west of Fredericksburg. On December 12, 1862, Burnside launched his attack against murderous fire from the Confederates, and on December 15 he recalled his troops from the field under cover of a heavy fog. Severely beaten, the Federals had lost 12,653 men; the Confederates, approximately 5,000. The news of this battle must

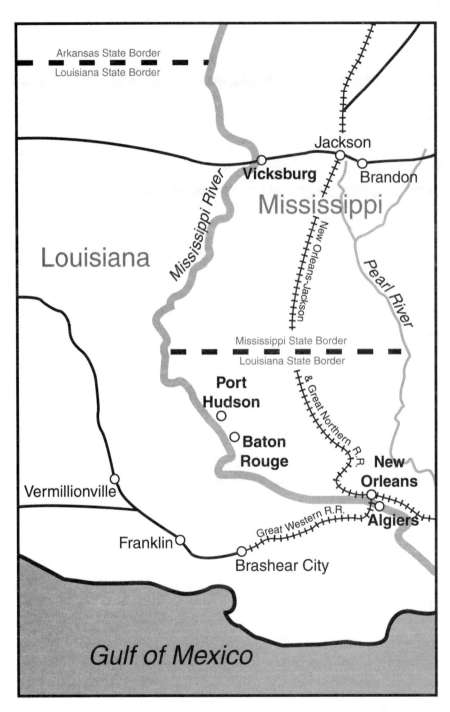

The Mississippi corridor in contention in early 1863

Drawn by Jim Robinson, Beidel Printing House, Inc.

have had a sobering effect on all of the Federal units training at Camp Joe Hooker.

The men at Camp Hooker were mastering the art of marching and review. It was not an easy task for a group of factory workers from Massachusetts who may have marched only once or twice in a hometown parade. The drills were fairly complicated with a prescribed number of paces and specific positions for officers, members of the band, and the companies. Inspections were made of arms, dress, ammunition boxes, and knapsacks upon the command of the captain of the company. There was one dress parade daily with the band playing and flags flying. Firearms were to be kept clean, and ammunition kept dry and accounted for. There was little spare time, yet despite the regimentation and new military lifestyle, only a couple of men were sent home due to disability. Approximately 15 men changed their minds about army service and deserted.

By mid-December assignments for the new units had been determined. The 4th Massachusetts Infantry Regiment was on its way to the Mississippi River area of New Orleans. Their commander would be General Nathaniel Banks, a native of Massachusetts, who was elected governor in 1858, and appointed to the position of major general of volunteers by President Lincoln in 1861. General Banks was first and foremost a politician who could rouse his native state to great heights of patriotism. Military command was not one of his areas of expertise as evidenced by his record in the Shenandoah Valley campaign of 1862. Stonewall Jackson had defeated him throughout the valley with the end result that General Banks lost 30 percent of his forces. However, General Banks was appointed commander of the Department of the Gulf in the winter of 1862, to replace General Benjamin Butler.[1]

General Butler was from New England and had been appointed military governor of Louisiana when New Orleans fell to the Union troops in April 1862. His administration was less than effective and a constant source of irritation to the citizens of Louisiana. He was accused of selling confiscated cotton as well as any other items he could appropriate for his own personal gain. In the South his nickname was Beast Butler as a result of his "Woman's Order" which stated that the women of New Orleans must stop insulting Union occupation troops or be treated as ladies of the street. This was not well accepted by the North or South, and clearly President Lincoln needed to remove General Butler from the Gulf command. When General Butler was advised that he was being replaced, he ordered all of the distilleries within his command closed as he anticipated a great deal of revelry. General Banks arrived in New Orleans on December 16, 1862, and took over as commander while the 4th Massachusetts Infantry Regiment trained at Lakeville, Massachusetts.[2]

Transportation was arranged to move the Lakeville recruits to the Gulf. On Saturday, December 27, 1862, they left Camp Hooker by ship for New York City to await passage to New Orleans. There were rough seas, and Private Walter S. Riddell, Company B, was evidently washed overboard and drowned before the ship reached the New York port.

If the passage from Boston had been difficult, the regiment faced an even greater challenge aboard the ship assigned to take them south to the New Orleans area. They were billeted on the ship *George Peabody*, a contract vessel, registered in 1854, to William F. Weld, William G. Weld, and Richard Baker Jr. all of Boston. Cornelius Vanderbilt acted as the special agent contracting transportation for the government. The ship was built in 1853, measured 190 feet, 2 inches long, 39 feet, 4 inches wide, and weighed 1,397 tons. John Manson was her master in 1854. By 1861, she was owned by the Powhatan Steam Boat Company of Baltimore, Maryland, with Thomas Travers as her master and berthed at New York City. The *George Peabody* was in a contract agreement with the United States War Department for $650 per day; her total value stated at $125,000. She had run aground in November 1862 at Hatteras Inlet, North Carolina, and the USS *Delaware* was dispatched from New Berne, North Carolina, to provide assistance. Evidently, there was no serious damage. Three months after she carried the 4th to New Orleans, the U.S. Quartermaster decided she was only acceptable for transporting horses.

Approximately seven hundred men of the 4th Massachusetts Infantry Regiment boarded the *George Peabody* on January 3, 1863. To relieve crowding, the remainder of the regiment, Company F, and segments of Companies A and I were transported aboard the *Alice Connee, Empire City,* and *Continental.* Even then the quarters of the *George Peabody* were tightly packed. The crew of the *George Peabody* was composed of 40 men, mostly foreign born, and the ship's officers. This crew only added to the miseries at the start of the trip by staging a short, but departure-delaying, mutiny. Another day was lost when the crew refused to sail on Friday, a sailor's superstition prevalent at that time.

The *George Peabody* reached Hampton Roads, Virginia, on January 8 and anchored at the mouth of the James River. It was cold and snowing but still better than tossing on the swells of the Atlantic Ocean. The soldiers were allowed to leave the ship on January 12 to visit Fort Monroe and drill on the beach while food and water were stored on board. One soldier from Company H died, and his remains were prepared to be shipped back to his family in Massachusetts.

On January 15 the *George Peabody* set sail and passed Cape Hatteras the following day. At least half of the men were too seasick to eat, and the quality of the food was so poor that it sickened those who were fortunate enough not to be seasick. They were at the mercy of the chilling winds on some days; on others, the sails hung slack as the ship mercilessly rocked back and forth on the waves. By the twenty-third they sighted the island of Abaco, and the weather became much milder.

The first entry in the diary is dated January 1863 and describes the voyage. The exact date and the first sentences are missing.

January ? *"...called the Dazs rocks—was in a very dangers situation. all the soldgers was ordered below. we was sailing in 18 feet of water. the ship then drawing [?] feet. got over it all safe."*

The diarist is most likely referring to Dog Rocks by the Cal Say Bank off the coast of Cuba in the Straits of Florida.

January 26 *"made Metanses light on the coast of Cuba."*

Matanzas is a town in Cuba across from Key West, Florida, where a lighthouse was located for ship guidance.

January 27 *"Exchanged signals from an English larte."*

Perhaps he is referring to a dory, a type of fishing boat with high sides. It is questionable since he refers to it as being an English ship, but it may have flown the Union Jack for protection during the blockade. Dargan's diary mentions passing a number of ships in this area just off the coast of Florida and Cuba.

January 28 *"Bad and squaly wether all day."*

January 29/30 *"calm wether."*

January 31 *"steady progress."*

While the men of the 4th Massachusetts Infantry Regiment tossed about on the sea, prominent military leaders were planning strategies that would influence the regiment's term of service. First, General Ulysses Simpson Grant, a West Point graduate of 1843 and a future president of the United States, had been appointed as a brigadier general of volunteers in

August 1861. By January 1863, his goal was to capture Vicksburg on the Mississippi River. Grant's first attempt in December 1862 had been repulsed by the Confederates.[3] Second, Admiral David Glasgow Farragut, whose fleet had been instrumental in the capture of New Orleans and Baton Rouge, was equally obsessed with opening the Mississippi River between New Orleans and Vicksburg.[4] Third, General Joseph Eggleston Johnston, of the Confederate army, was deeply involved in the struggle for the Mississippi corridor. A West Point graduate, he had seen considerable action in Virginia where he was wounded during May 1862 in the battle of Seven Pines. Unfortunately, General Johnston was also an object of political infighting in the Confederate army and had been given overall command of the Department of the West late in 1862. His main responsibilities were to supervise General Braxton Bragg in Tennessee and General John Clifford Pemberton at Vicksburg. It was a thankless assignment considering the Federal thrust to crush Vicksburg and Port Hudson on the Mississippi River corridor.[5]

The president of the United States and the president of the Confederacy were formulating their battle plans at the same time. In December 1862, President Jefferson Davis visited the Tennessee and Mississippi commands and was deeply concerned about the entire western theater. Some of the blame was certainly his since he had directed most of his efforts toward the conflicts in Maryland and Virginia. Governor John Jones Pettus of Mississippi accused Davis of frequently visiting the Army of Northern Virginia and of neglecting the problems in the west.[6]

The Federals had the advantage in numbers of men in the western theater, and Admiral Farragut's navy was far superior than that of the Confederates. Davis advised his secretary of war that the ironclads would be trouble in the Mississippi, and he wanted more effective armament. He also wired

General Pemberton at Vicksburg to inquire if he had been talking to General Johnston, an indication that communication and coordination efforts were not at a satisfactory level.

President Lincoln instructed General Banks that opening the Mississippi River was his first and most important assignment as Gulf commander. For Banks, with political aspirations, this was a golden opportunity to outshine General Grant, his junior in rank. However, Banks was not yet ready in January 1863. Washington waited and waited. Admiral Farragut was ready to move upriver, and he too questioned the delay. Banks was concerned because he maintained that he had an inadequate number of troops. In January the Confederates had 12,000 men at Port Hudson, and Banks had 36,000 men with many garrisoned throughout the lower Gulf area to guard, in Banks' opinion, strategic waterways. The *War of the Rebellion: A Compilation of the Official Records of the Union and Confederate Armies* for the entire campaign are sprinkled with Banks' concerns about troop levels and calls for additional support at all locations around the New Orleans area.

Despite the pressure from Washington, Banks decided to move more of his men west of the Mississippi to secure the Red River and Bayou Teche. This required even more men, thereby causing more delay while campaign plans were redrawn. Meanwhile, his army met opposition at Fort Bisland near Pattersonville and had to return to Brashear City. The bayous were flooded, the rivers were high, and the swamps allowed virtually no troop movement. Banks' western campaign plans were abandoned, and precious attack time on Port Hudson had been lost. This was not what President Lincoln or General in Chief Henry Wager Halleck wanted to see or to hear.

Concurrent to the military campaigns and conflicts, President Lincoln issued his Emancipation Proclamation Act on

January 1, 1863. The act stated that all slaves in rebellious
sections were free, but slaves in the border states loyal to the
Union were not. In fact, it took the 13th Amendment, passed
in December 1865, to completely outlaw slavery in the country.[7] The slaves of the Confederate states fled plantations and
farms seeking out the Union army and were accepted into army
service. It was a far cry from the previous August when free
Negroes sought to join the army and were rejected. In reality,
it took several months to organize Negro regiments. The 4th
Massachusetts Infantry Regiment eventually fought side by
side with Negro troops at Port Hudson, where for the first
time Negro regiments were assigned to assault positions.

Chapter III

February 1863
Encampment in Louisiana

The Civil War was slowly grinding onward. There was limited activity in the Virginia theater due to the winter weather, but the Army of the Potomac had a new commander, General Joseph Hooker. President Lincoln was still plagued by the need for a strong department commander and the jockeying for position among members of his general staff. General Banks, convinced he was without a large enough army to launch a serious offensive against Port Hudson, deployed his troops across the Gulf area. Many of them spent the month of February clearing Bayou Plaquemine of logs and debris to open it for navigation.

The Confederate commander of Port Hudson made excellent use of Banks' delay by reinforcing his garrison and establishing new defensive positions. General Franklin Gardner assumed command of Port Hudson late in 1862. Gardner was born in New York City and was in the same class as General Grant at West Point. Married into a Louisiana family, his sympathies were entirely with the Confederacy, while a brother served in the Union army. Gardner, who served in Mexico and never formally resigned from the U.S. Army, was appointed a lieutenant colonel in the Confederate army in March 1861 and was dropped from the rolls of the U.S. Army in May of the same year.[1]

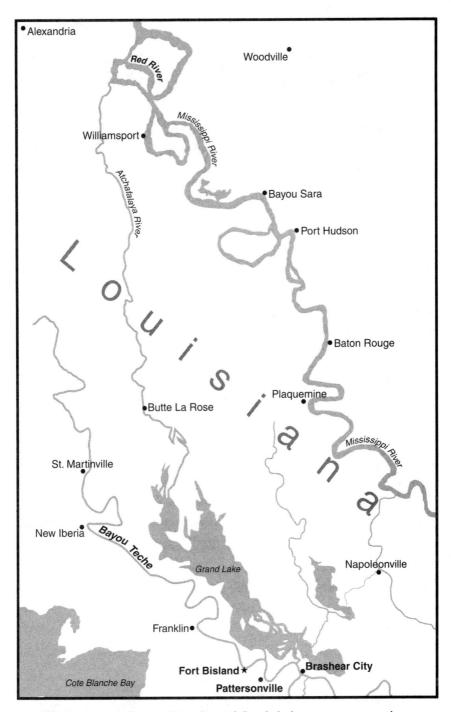

The area of General Nathaniel Banks' thrust to secure the southwestern portion of Louisiana in late 1862 and early 1863

Drawn by Jim Robinson, Beidel Printing House, Inc.

February found the troops of the 4th Massachusetts Infantry still living onboard the *George Peabody*. The diary continues:

February 1 *"inspection of regiment."*
This was probably the first time inspection was held since they left Massachusetts. High seas and very cold weather would not have allowed this routine very frequently.

February 2 *"dead calm all day."*

That night the band played on the ship's deck in an attempt to relieve the monotony, but strong winds came up abruptly sending everyone below for shelter. The sailors, evidently a superstitious lot, remarked that music aboard the ship always brought a "hard blow."

February 3 *"High wind all night. Pilot took aboard at Pilottown at night. Stemer Anglou American towed us up the river about 15 miles, then gave out. Still at ancor the river running about 8 miles an hour. This night was very could [cold] most froze in our bunk. Ice in the buckets next morning."*
The steamer the diarist is referring to is the Union steamer *Anglo American*, which had been running the Mississippi in the summer of 1862 under the command of Captain P. K. Riley. In August and September 1862, she had been fired upon from Port Hudson. In June 1863, she would be commanded by Captain Cole and be on fire at Plaquemine between New Orleans and Springfield Landing, the result of an attack by Texas cavalry.

February 6 *"Started up the river about noon. The sun a little warmer. Kept running all night."*

At dusk on the sixth, the ship reached Point Quarantine north of Fort Jackson on the Mississippi River. Two men of the 4th were left there suffering from some form of illness.

The gravestones scattered around the post area were grim indicators of what might be ahead.

February 7   *"Came to ancor about five miles below Orleans opposite the nunerse [?]."*

This was probably another troop ship, again phonetically spelled, which still remains unidentified.

February 8   *"Sunday service on board. Still at ancor."*

February 9   *"Still at ancor in the river, wether mild."*

February 10   *"Still at ancor. The ship Jenny Lims past us with the 50 Mass on board."*

This was the ship *Jenny Lind*, carrying three companies and headquarters personnel of the 50th Massachusetts Infantry Regiment. The men of the 4th Regiment were not allowed to disembark the ship while it was at anchor causing, as one would expect, a great deal of grumbling. Some tempers flared, and there was at least one incident of a struggle among the troops and the ship's crew.

February 11   *"Towed up the river past Orleans to Carrolton about 15 miles. Landed at the wharf at Carrolton at noon. The sailors was searched for things stolen from the soldgers. All the things found. Tride to make ther escape at night was stoped by the garde."*

The ship had arrived at Carrollton, Louisiana. Not only did the regiment have a long and rough trip, they were also preyed upon by the hands aboard the *George Peabody*.

February 12   *"The sailors was taken to prison."*

February 13   *"Left the ship* George Peabody *and to come to sleep on her at night. There was nobody in the camp the ground being wet."*

Finally, after 47 days aboard ship, the 4th Massachusetts Infantry Regiment reached their destination. They were to be stationed at Camp Mansfield near Carrollton, Louisiana. Between the end of January and the March 31, several troop transports arrived at this same destination.

Some of these were:

Montebello—Three companies of the 5th Massachusetts and 250 convalescents

Constellation—The 48th Massachusetts Regiment

Jennie Beals—The 25th New York Battery rescued from the wreck of the *Sparkling Sea*. All horses had been lost at sea

E. Wilder Farley—The 12th Massachusetts Battery

Illinois—The 49th Massachusetts Regiment plus four companies, and headquarters personnel of the 21st Maine. Also, Brigadier General Andrews and Brigadier General Dwight

William Woodbury—The 176th New York, and 2 officers, and 72 enlisted men of the 4th Massachusetts. The men of the 4th had been transferred from the *Alice Connee*, in Hampton Roads, Virginia

Crescent—Company F, 2nd Rhode Island Cavalry

Jenny Lind—The 50th Massachusetts troops which had passed the *George Peabody* on February 10

Belle Wood—Company C, 2nd Rhode Island Cavalry

Undaunted—Companies B and D of the 2nd Rhode Island Cavalry

Empire City and the *Continental*—The remainder of the 4th Massachusetts, perhaps 30 men, and other unidentified units

General George Andrews, born in Bridgewater, Massachusetts, attended West Point and graduated at the head of his class. Appointed brigadier general of volunteers in 1862, he had seen action in Virginia and Maryland, notably at Antietam. His duty in Louisiana was chief of staff for General

Banks. Later in his career he would oversee the training of Negro troops recruited from the Mississippi area.[2]

General William Dwight was a fellow New Englander born in Springfield, Massachusetts, who attended West Point but never graduated. Dwight saw action at Williamsburg, Virginia, where he was wounded and captured by the Confederates. Exchanged shortly thereafter, he was sent to Louisiana to command a brigade for General Banks.[3]

The 4th Massachusetts Infantry Regiment was assigned to the 1st Brigade, 3rd Division, XIX Corps. General William Hemsley Emory, the division commander, was born in Queen Anne County, Maryland, and graduated from West Point in 1831. Emory had an excellent record in the Mexican War and as a topographical engineer was active in surveying the country west of the Mississippi including California and Mexico. Emory was charged with defending New Orleans during the Port Hudson campaign.[4]

The brigade was commanded by Colonel Timothy Ingraham of the 28th Massachusetts. Ingraham, also from New England, was 50 years old when the Civil War began. Originally assigned to command the 3rd Brigade, Ingraham was transferred to the 1st Brigade and served through the spring of 1863. Ill health forced him to return to Washington, D.C., to serve as provost marshal. The commission of brevet brigadier general was awarded to Ingraham on October 2, 1865, one day before he was mustered out of the U.S. Army.

The brigade was composed of the 4th Massachusetts Infantry, the 16th New Hampshire and the 110th and 162nd New York Infantry Regiments. The 4th Massachusetts Infantry Regiment left Louisiana in August 1863, while the 110th and the 162nd New York Regiments stayed on. In September of 1863, the majority of these two regiments had what was commonly known as "swamp fever," but more likely it was malaria.[5]

Approximately 15,000 troops, mostly nine-month men, were shipped to the Gulf to serve under General Banks. By early spring of 1863, he would have approximately 30,000 men organized in four divisions representing the XIX Corps. Fifty-six regiments were represented, 22 of which were nine-month men with enlistments expiring in May, July, and August 1863.

In early February, one of the most active Union rams, *Queen of the West*, passed the Confederate batteries at Vicksburg during daylight hours. She was hit 12 times but continued on to capture three Confederate ships south of Vicksburg. By the tenth of February the *Queen* had moved down the Mississippi River heading for the Red River with Commodore David Dixon Porter in command of the gunboat fleet. The *Queen* arrived at the Red River, ran aground on February 14, and was subsequently abandoned. Later she was repaired by the Confederates and saw use in the area flying the Confederate flag.

By the third week in February, Port Hudson, having been fortified by the Confederates, accounted for 16,000 men. (General Banks estimated the Confederate force to be 18,000 men.) Confederates were also based at several locations on the Bayou Teche. At Pattersonville, Fort Bisland, and Berwick Bay to Alexandria and Grand Encore, there were probably 12,000 to 15,000 Confederate soldiers.

General Banks, who had dispatched troops to numerous parts of the Gulf area, had 12,000 to 14,000 troops available to launch the attack on Port Hudson. His campaign plan was to deploy troops to the Atchafalaya River and Bayou Teche, so gunboats could patrol the Red River and cut supply channels to the Confederates at Port Hudson and Vicksburg.

Admiral Farragut, who had lost the *Queen of the West* and had difficulty moving ships past Port Hudson, disagreed with General Banks' plans. Farragut wanted to develop a concentrated effort of ground and river forces to clear the Mississippi River by capturing Port Hudson and moving upriver to support General Grant at Vicksburg. Essentially he wanted to stay out of the back country and attack the major river fortifications. The Red River was, indeed, a supply line for the Confederates but of little use if there were no strongholds left to support.

The diary continues:

February 14   *"Sleep on land for the first time since we left camp Joe Horter* [Hooker]*."*

February 15   *"Nothing new."*

There were some "new" happenings—downpours and mud. The rain penetrated the men's tents and flooded their sleeping areas. Dargan refers to the "nasty, sticky, putty mud that can take your boots off quicker than any boot jack in the country."[6]

February 16   *"Had gard mounting for the first time in L.A. We was camped along the side of the 49th. Col. Bartlett— they got orders to move at night—laughable caus this night fore* [four] *men fell in the back house—got covered all over head—bad smell."*

February 18   *"the band pladed for a funeral, Private F. Conn."*

This is the diarist's first reference to his band activity. In war, death becomes so commonplace that men often lose their identities and become just one more casualty. There were six Connecticut regiments in the XIX Corps, but the diarist identifies the deceased only by rank, initial, and state.

February 19   *"I went down to New Orleans to the trial of the sailors as a witness   they   was found guilty...30 days in prison. I whent to the new custom house then I met Alis Warner and lots mor I knew. I had time to travel."*

The diarist is probably referring to a civil trial for the sailors on the *George Peabody*, a contract vessel not under military law. The name of Warner to whom he refers may be Alexander Warner of the 26th Maine Regiment in the 2nd Brigade, 3rd Division, XIX Corps. Warner was born in England and was approximately the same age as the probable author of this diary. He was from Lawrence, Massachusetts, and unfortunately died in later life at a hospital for the insane.

The reference to "I had time to travel" may be indicative of limited-duty assignment. Dargan indicates in his diary that he had time on his hands. He spent much of that period touring the area and talking to fellow soldiers.[7]

February 21   *"New Orleans eight hours. The regiment at the first dress parade since we left Massctusts."*

The regiment is back to practicing the general orders prescribed by the U.S. Army. It probably was comfortable wearing their woolen uniforms in February although it may have been warming up along the river. In a few weeks these same uniforms would be soaked in sweat as the heat and humidity set in.

February 27   *"Gard mountin* [mounting] *changed from nine in the morning till 3 in the afternoon."*

Although the author of the diary never mentions animosity among the men enlisted for three years versus those in the nine-month units, Dargan comments several times about the bad feelings created by the length-of-service discrepancy. He was also very critical of the regimental hospital services and was sure men died because of the medical treatment they received. That was not an unusual statement as many Civil War historical books echo the same sentiments.

It was a whole new world for these men from Massachusetts, who had endured a long, cramped, filthy existence on the *George Peabody*. The penetrating, cold damp was much different from a New England winter. They had seen the grave sites that resulted from battle and disease, and although they had not yet experienced either, they were aware that they would eventually experience both.

Chapter IV

March 1863
Misery and Marching

On March 3 another member of the 4th Massachusetts died and was laid to rest in Louisiana soil. The burial occurred by moonlight with two brothers of the deceased, who were also members of the regiment, attending the service.

The first diary entry for March is dated the first Thursday of the month.

March 5   *"receded orders to move at 5 minutes notice at any day."*

Admiral Farragut was bringing pressure to bear on General Banks in demanding there be a concentrated effort against Port Hudson. As long as the batteries were in place at the Confederate fort, U.S. gunboats were threatened and could not move north to Vicksburg to assist General Grant in his campaign. General Banks was still convinced his troop strength was not adequate for ground attack, but he knew he could stall no longer.

The plan called for a ground demonstration against Port Hudson while the naval fleet attempted to run the Confederate batteries. All available army troops were to move to Baton Rouge in early March. General Banks' official report concerning preparations for this engagement indicates the ground attack was not to be full-scale, only diversionary. He was cooperating with Admiral Farragut and meeting Washington

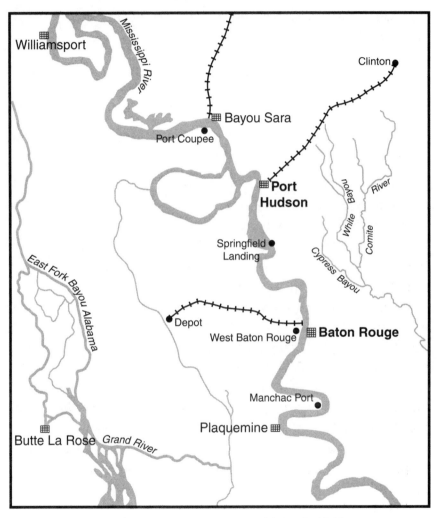

Troop deployment area in mid-March 1863, as
Admiral David Farragut ran the Port Hudson fortifications

Drawn by Jim Robinson, Beidel Printing House, Inc.

directives, but obviously, he was not yet committed to an all-out attack. Admiral Farragut evidently thought some action was better than none and agreed to the plan.

March 6 *"broke up camp to go board the Lurel Hill sleept on board in the rain."*

March 7 *"Set sail up the river to Baton Rouge the wether was plesent country looked deserted nothing to be seen on the banks but help [half] naked nigors badly clothed."*

March 8 *"landed at Baton Rouge whent to camp about three about 8 miles from the city."*

There appears to be a sense of renewed interest in his surroundings as the diary's author records almost every day in March. He could not have known that all these preparations would produce a dismal failure. This would be his first battle, and one can only surmise the level of excitement and anticipation, perhaps even the chilling feelings of fear.

The Confederates were aware of the Federal's plans and were on alert. Not only did they have scouts in the area, but friendly plantation owners were also quick to supply intelligence. General Franklin Gardner continually fortified his positions, and on the same day the diary's author entered camp at Baton Rouge, Gardner opened a levee below Port Hudson. This would prevent U.S. troops from attacking below the fort. Conditions at Port Hudson were difficult, but morale was high even though the Confederates overestimated the strength of the Federal forces Banks would deploy.

March 9 *"We receved orders to be in readnes to move in light marching order but did not go for some time."*

March 10 *"the same order as on the 9."*

Banks had issued orders on the night of March 8, but the coordination of the attack did not go smoothly. The ground troops needed to wait for the navy to get into position for the river assault. Admiral Farragut, in direct command of the operation, left nothing to chance. His fleet consisted of at least five gunboats with a backup reserve of another four, plus six mortar schooners. All of the ships were heavily armed and fortified to eliminate severe damage from Confederate shelling. Although such preparation requires time and effort, the prime reason for Farragut's delay was that he was awaiting repairs on the *Essex*. She was to be brought up to Baton Rouge and used as naval support to protect Banks' rear once Farragut passed Port Hudson. General Banks refused to move his troops until he believed he was secure from being cut off from New Orleans. As a result the attack date was delayed.

Advance infantry skirmishers and cavalry patrols had already been dispatched, leaving many men standing in the mud and rain awaiting further orders. Darkness brought so much confusion that Federal units fired on each other. Again, Banks' already questionable determination began to waver based on a rumor that the Confederate army in Virginia was moving towards the Mississippi River. The Union troops conducted a furious bridge-burning effort on the Comite River to protect the rear and flank of the troops at Baton Rouge, but the Army of Northern Virginia was nowhere in the area.[1]

March 11   *"Got more marching orders with seven days rachen in our haversacks and 3 in teems to be ready in five minutes notice."*

The frustration level of the troops must have been very high as they waited to enter battle. Admiral Farragut arrived in Baton Rouge aboard the *Essex* on March 11. The army was on alert and partially deployed, but the navy was not yet ready to move. The soldiers did not know that Farragut was delayed because he had to meet more demands of General Banks.

March 12   *"grand reveue under Gen Banks."*

Marching orders were held in abeyance by General Banks in order to stage a grand review of his command. Perhaps it was to impress Admiral Farragut and his staff, but it is difficult to understand how either commander agreed to suspend all activity for a military show. There was undoubtedly pride in the Federal troops as they stood at attention, but many thoughts must have been on the seven-day rations molding in their haversacks.[2]

On March 13 the first serious deployment of troops began. Two Massachusetts units, excluding the 4th Massachusetts Infantry, embarked to Springfield Landing via gunboats. Cavalry moved to intercept Confederate pickets while other New England and New York units established themselves at a bridge on Cypress Bayou.

General Emory's division, including the 4th Massachusetts Infantry, was part of the main column supported by General Cuvier Grover's 4th Division and General Christopher Augur's 1st Division. Both Grover and Augur were West Point graduates and career army men. Before being assigned to the Department of the Gulf, they were active in Federal campaigns in Virginia. The column advanced up the Bayou Sara Road to Plank Road towards Clinton making side feints where necessary to clear Confederate defenders. Taking no chances, General Banks left behind some three thousand men to protect his rear at Baton Rouge.

March 13   *"left Baton Rouge towards Port Hudson   Set of* [off] *at seven o clock at night   We travel 8 miles   we thru up our shalters* [shelter] *tents for the first time."*

Emory's division experienced a long, dusty, and very warm night. An eight-mile march would have taken them to the vicinity of White Bayou. Exhaustion was prevalent, the moldy seven-day rations gave no solace, and the woolen uniforms were hot and damp from sweat.

March 14   *"We left camp an we traveld on about 4 miles Then we alted* [altered] *to let some calverlemen and general Banks   Then we proced towards the Clinton Road were we come up to the mims Battery* [Ormand F. Nims Battery] *and got orders to camp for the night   forragein* [foraging] *took place for the first time   We camped all night without alarm."*

General Emory's division was up at 3 A.M. but did not march for another four hours. The day became hotter by the minute, and discarded equipment soon began to litter the roadside. As General Banks rode by, there were mixed acknowledgments, a few cheers, but mostly silence. Water was supplied by stagnant puddles, canteens having been drained hours before. Hundreds of men became candidates for dysentery, typhoid, and malaria.

Most of the advancing Federal troops had stopped by late afternoon on the fourteenth. There were numerous skirmishes in these two days resulting in deaths and woundings. Admiral Farragut advised General Banks at 5 P.M. on March 14 that he intended to "run" Port Hudson that night. Fog had prevented his passage on the morning of the fourteenth, but he thought the diversion created by the ground forces was an effective maneuver. Banks did not get into position on time the afternoon of the fourteenth and made no attempt to cover Farragut's naval movement.

Admiral Farragut did indeed "run" Port Hudson. He lost the *Monongahela*, the *Richmond*, and the *Mississippi*. There were to be four congressional Medal of Honor recipients on the gunboat *Richmond,* plus scores of tales of bravery. The Confederates responded to Farragut's run on the Mississippi with equal bravery and loss of life. It was a long, bloody night while the Union army lie in their respective camps listening to the bombardment but unable to be of any assistance.[3]

Farragut was able to get two ships above Port Hudson on the Mississippi. Not a great Union victory, but a move that could severely disrupt Confederate supply lines at the Red River. Two ships could not blockade the Mississippi between Port Hudson and Vicksburg, but the Confederate lifeline was slowly being severed. Perhaps if Banks had pushed his ground forces to advance on Port Hudson to create the diversionary conditions that were part of the original plan, the situation may have been very different. The Confederates would have been occupied on both land and water, greatly taxing their capabilities.

The Union army started to their rear on March 15, most not knowing what transpired during the night. There was an element of fear since this was essentially a retreat and would indicate that Farragut had been defeated, while the Confederates moved across the bayou country. However, word travels fast in an army, and the foot soldiers soon learned Farragut had passed Port Hudson with very little help from them.

March 15   *"a general forrage took place   hens pigs sweet potatoes beef stacikae* [steak] *and sheep   we got orders to fall 2 miles   Camped close to the forth eight* [48th Mass] *2 camps Captain Shearman   We pitched tents   it began to rain forragein goin on   Horses Mules   The rain now fell in torrents Some of the men lay in the water   Some stud up all night."*

March 16   *"Marched back to the pontons bridge."*

March 17   *"Marched back to Clinton Cross roads   Whent to bed at eight   rose at 12 feel* [fell] *back 3 miles to another Brigade."*

From the diary entries, it appears that local farm and plantation owners paid their dues to the Union army. There could not have been much livestock left behind after the three army divisions passed through. The diary notations of the fifteenth, sixteenth, and seventeenth also indicate that there was some crisscrossing and backward movement during the retreat. The following entries express similar movement.[4]

March 18   *We marched back to the pontoon bridge at night when [went] throw [through] a dark swamp nee deep in water and old trees lain all a cross."*

March 19   *"fair day rested in camp all day and night."*

March 20   *"Marched back to Baton Rouge at ½ past 5 got in Baton Rouge at 9 o'clock at night   tired out   acted the rear gard for the whole army   Thus ended the Port Hudson affair."*

March 24   *"Moved camp at Baton Rouge near the city."*
It appears there were two or three days of rest and inactivity, and certainly it must have been a welcome change.

March 26   *"The band went to the presenting of a flag to the 133 New York by Billy Wilson   The band got jolly drunk   I fell on my horne [horn]   got to camp at night all safe."*
The 133rd New York was part of General Emory's division and had been part of the Port Hudson campaign. Billy Wilson was the commander of the 6th New York National Guard Infantry Regiment, whose members enlisted for the duration of the war. Members took the oath on bended knee at Tammany Hall in New York City. Dargan's diary notes that the men of the 6th showed nothing but contempt for the nine-month enlistees. Despite a very difficult month, the routine of army life fell into place, and the author of the diary woke up the next morning with a hangover![5]

March 27   *"feel a little sick after the sleep."*

March 28   *"hard rain all night   very hard till morning The camp fluded."*

March 31   *"A brigade review by Genl Ingerham [Ingraham] first rate day."*

The organization roster of the troops in the Department of the Gulf dated April 30, 1863, recorded Ingraham as having the rank of lieutenant colonel. Ingraham had, however, succeeded Brigadier General George L. Andrews, so it was a natural mistake on the part of the diarist to refer to Ingraham as a general.

The regiment's first active campaign was over. In a military sense it had been very unproductive. Yet, the men had experienced their first taste of war, complete with its confusion, hardships, anxiety, and unquestionable orders.

Chapter V

April 1863
Fort Bisland

For some reason the author of the diary becomes more verbose during the month of April. Perhaps this is because he was involved in his first real encounter and some of the boredom of everyday army life had been dispelled. At Port Hudson, in March, he did not mention shooting, but in mid-April he was involved in an engagement at Fort Bisland, southwest of New Orleans, where his company was on the front lines.

April 1 *"all fools day   fooling in camp."*

April 2 *"got orders to march down river   struck tents and put them up again for the night   The boat not being ready."*

April 3 *"got aboard the Schtea [?] at 9 o'clock   got to Algeres [Algiers] about sun set   landed pitched tents for the night   very hevy dew and cold that night."*

April 3, 1863, was Good Friday. Even with his phonetic spelling it is difficult to identify the name of the ship, but Dargan refers to boarding the *Natchez.* There was a gunboat named the *Sachem,* which may have been used temporarily for troop transport. It is highly probable that the army used several vessels. Interestingly enough, Dargan refers to this troop movement as the start of a Texas expedition. Moving into Texas was really what Banks wanted to initiate. Washington absolutely did not want that, and Grant thought it was

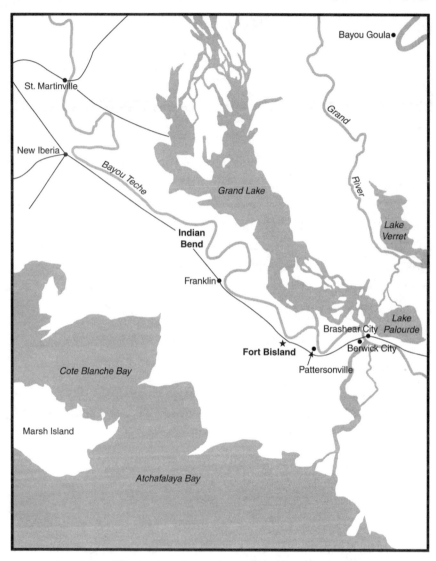

Area of the Fort Bisland campaign, April 1863

Drawn by Jim Robinson, Beidel Printing House, Inc.

courting disaster. The troops, however, must have picked up the Texas rumor from their officers.[1]

The troops landed at Algiers, located directly across the Mississippi River from New Orleans. Algiers was a busy military port during the Civil War. Not only did it access the river, it was also the start of a railroad line terminating at Brashear City. Prior to the Federals capturing New Orleans it was the site of the Confederate government's shipyards.

April 5 *"Sunday   Coly* [Colby] *had services at his tent acted as Chaplin."*

This was Easter Sunday, 1863. Lieutenant Colonel Ebenezer Colby, 3rd Division, 1st Brigade, reported to Colonel Timothy Ingraham. Colby, from Lawrence, Massachusetts, was a staff officer with the 4th Massachusetts Infantry Regiment. His direct-reporting line would have been to Colonel Henry Walker from Quincy, Massachusetts, but Colonel Walker was not on duty due to illness. Many in the 4th Massachusetts thought Walker was avoiding active duty by feigning poor health. It was also rumored that he drank heavily, which was the real reason he was not in command.

April 6 *"at brigade drill in the afternoon I whent to New Orleans   That I had a good looke round the city. Saw Brother Macfarland   Alec Warner got a pass   we whent thru the city He come with me to the ferre* [ferry] *boat   took sick and he had to go back   and dress parade that night   got marching orders with two days rachens."*

Alec Warner appears to be the same man referred to previously in the diary. Brother MacFarland may be Nahum McFarland of the 4th Massachusetts Infantry Regiment, Company I. (His last name on the regimental records is spelled incorrectly.) McFarland survived the war and died in Dover, New Hampshire, in 1912.

The preparation of rations signaled the beginning of a move by Federal troops against Confederate forces at Fort Bisland and along the Teche and Atchafalaya Rivers. Banks was now traveling west and north heading for Alexandria on the Red River. He was still concerned about Confederate concentrations in the bayou country and considered them to be a real threat to New Orleans and Baton Rouge. Essentially, he abandoned any drive on Port Hudson for almost two months and concerned himself with an area he had deemed dangerous since his arrival as commanding officer of the Department of the Gulf.

April 7 *"Cooking all day struck tents   Slept in our shelter tents   large fires at night."*

April 8 *"Left Algers and roade on the cars to within 4 miles of Brachaer* [Brashear] *City   rode in baggage cars   Plenty of alegators seen in the swamps   got of* [off] *the cars at three o'clock   slept in a corn* [cane] *brake that night."*

The Great Western Railroad ran between Algiers and Brashear City on the Bayou Teche River. Directly across the river from Brashear City was a smaller settlement known as Berwick City. The Bayou Teche follows a serpentine course not unlike the Mississippi and empties into the Gulf of Mexico. Most of the terrain along the railroad line and north along the river was swamp land. Brashear City was named for a large plantation owner and was renamed Morgan City in 1876.

Two forts were located on the bend of the Bayou Teche at Berwick, originally built by the Confederates, but now in the hands of the Federals. Beyond these two strongholds the country was Confederate territory.

April 9 *"Marched up to Brachaer City camp   A and K decked out on duty   pitched camp in Brachaer City that night."*

A and K refers to Companies A and K of the 4th Massachusetts Infantry.

April 10   *"still the same."*

April 11   *"left Bracher City at 6 PM   crossed the river on the luriel Hill* [Laurel Hill]   *started to march to our brigade got up to them ½ past two on Sunday   13 miles."*

April 12   *"rose up at 5 got   orders to throw pickets out in the wood   Saw rebels picket behind trees   followed them up when they let go ther artillery on us. We returned to them pretty sharp   the plan of battle was now for me by General Banks General Ingerham   be in the reserve withe his brigade   The battle commence at 3 o'clock   lasted till 20 minutes past fore* [four] *when our forces fell back for want of amenishon* [ammunition] *The rebels cheered greatly   Thus ended the first day."*

The march on April 11 would have placed the regiment at Pattersonville, a small settlement on one of Bayou Teche's many bends and only a few miles from the rebel-held Fort Bisland. Captain George S. Merrill's reports state that his unit was to reinforce General Emory's division, which was already facing the Confederates.

It took the better part of three days for the 4th Massachusetts to depart Brashear City and get into a support position in the front of Fort Bisland. The delay was due to the lack of adequate transportation for the troops to cross Berwick Bay on the Bayou Teche. Transports crossed, returned, and crossed again, a slow process until all of the men were finally in position on April 12.

While the 4th Massachusetts was getting into position, General Grover's troops were placed on transports to traverse the Atchafalaya and Grand Lake to land at Indian Bend a few miles beyond Fort Bisland. This action was also delayed because the shoreline waters of Grand Lake were very shallow, and the men had to be transferred to flatboats for the ground landing. In all, including a segment of troops moving by land, Banks commanded approximately 17,000 men on his drive against the Confederates who were commanded by General Richard Taylor.

General Richard Taylor was the son of President Zachary Taylor and a brother of the first wife of Jefferson Davis. Richard Taylor graduated from Yale in 1845, and became a plantation owner in Louisiana where he was very active in state politics. At the onset of the Civil War he was a colonel in the 9th Louisiana Infantry and was made brigadier general by mid-1862.[2]

Taylor's troop concentration in the Bayou Teche area probably did not exceed four thousand men. His advantage lay in the fact that he commanded Texas and Louisiana men who knew the area, were accustomed to swamps, could exist in the heat, and were protecting "home ground." There was strong motivation to keep the Yankees out of the western part of Louisiana, for they had already been far too successful in conquering a great deal of Louisiana. The Texas border invasion was unthinkable.

Taylor's line on April 12 consisted of 39 pieces of artillery and four thousand armed Confederates. The Confederate *Official Records* state that the skirmish began around 4:30 P.M., and darkness brought an end to the hostilities. These time frames are not too far off from those expressed in the diary. The Texas cavalry was under the command of Brigadier General Henry Sibley, a hard-drinking officer with a questionable performance record that eventually led to a court-martial hearing. He graduated from West Point in 1838, invented the Sibley tent used by both sides during the first years of the Civil War, and after the war, went to Egypt to serve in the Egyptian army.[3] The night of April 12, General Taylor made a reconnaissance to establish the location of General Grover's troops. Sibley was instructed to move his brigade at sunrise on the thirteenth against Banks' left. Sibley, left on his own, did not follow Taylor's instructions to launch a counterattack, so the next move was up to the Federals.[4]

The following entries in the diary are very carefully written, and the pages begin with the title, "Days Fight at Camp
Bislaner." This campaign evidently made a deep impression
upon the diary's author.

April 13   *"the fight comnenced at nine o clock morning
Three Brigeades lay before the enmys brest works 6 hundred
yards apart   our brigead suported the Indiana Battery   the
fight whent on about even for fore hours   The fire became more
quick now then anytime befor 1 oclock for about half hour when
the fire slachen* [slacken] *again at fore oclock   it sprong up
again with renewed vigor."*

*"Our infantry met some smart musketery   could be heard
to our left   the fight becam general   now the yell of the Texas
men could be heard   Then the hurrar* [hurrah] *of our boys
could be heard in the wood to the left   The rebels was trying to
take some of our bras* [artillery] *peces but got met with a volly
of musketery that sent them back to the strong hold to be seen
no more   our wounded began to come in prity fast   Some of the
regular Battery lost 3 killed five wounded and fore horses killed
The 4* [?] *regement lost some dead and wounded   The 8 New
Hampshire the 114 New York and a number of others   I saw
five dead and 15 wounded   The sun set and the fight ceasced
as if by mutual concent   The advance of our colom fell back for
to rest at night   The 4 Mass was sent up to within the enemey
brest works to stop   Ther all night   These men could heer the
rebels talking very plane   A few shots ware* [were] *fired at the
4 but they was pronn* [prone] *on the belleys so that the shots
went over   The 4 fired 4 shots that night thinking they saw
something aprochin   no sleep for thes boys and al stud in the
battle field all the day before but before morning the forth Mass
could hear the rebels retreating and at day light all left ther."*

The 4th Massachusetts, although heavily engaged,
reported no dead or wounded. The 4th Regiment he refers to

as having dead and wounded men was probably the 4th Wisconsin.

April 14 *"stron [strong] works and we took poseion of them we followed them up prety close   took prisoners to the amount of 250   then our army took Franklin that night   still the enemy was still in full retreat   our army did drove more than 21 miles that day   I lost my regement that day   Joined at next day   our regement was ordered back to Brasher City and to take two hundred horses and mules   Col. Colby still commanding."*

Franklin is north of Fort Bisland and slightly south of where General Grover was landing his troops by flatboats on Grand Lake. Banks' plan had been to place Federal troops at Fort Bisland in General Taylor's front, attack, and cut off Taylor's escape route back along the Bayou Teche. General Grover's landing was the important part, but his troop deployment was delayed and after landing at Grand Lake he went into camp. Taylor deployed a small group of cavalry to harass Grover's forward movement, and on the morning of the fourteenth, Taylor's cavalry attacked the Federals. The element of surprise allowed enough time for Taylor to move the main elements of his army by General Grover and escape northward. Taylor burned the gunboat *Diana*, which had continually shelled Federal troops during the Fort Bisland encounter to keep her out of Federal hands and torched a number of bridges on his retreat.[5]

Banks' attack plan was a good one. Only timing destroyed its effectiveness, and Taylor, although greatly outnumbered, was still at large to cause the Federals future trouble. This would be very evident in the month of June 1863.

April 15 *"The regement traveled eight miles that day and settled for the night in a very pretty place and piched our tents   all troops gone only and we was on our road to hold Brasher City."*

April 16   "*Marched back past Patsonville* [Pattersonville]
met Col. Walker this [——] *had been withe the regement since
the 3 of April   he had been sick   he then took command   all the
men in the regement did not like him and they wished he had
stayed away.*"

Colonel Walker evidently rejoined his regiment early in
April but was not in command during the Fort Bisland affair.
On April 14 the diary's author states Colonel Colby was still
in command.

April 17   "*Marched to Berwick City opposit Brasher City
we crosed the river in the Southern Merchant   got some of our
men arested for firing ther pecis* [pieces] *in the water.*"

April 18   "*Comps* [companies] *A and C is ordered down
to the fort   Comp* [?] *and G at the depot.*"

The fort would have been Fort Buchanan. The depot he
refers to is at the terminus of the Great Western Railroad at
Brashear City. Dargan describes Brashear City in his diary
as only having seven or eight houses but a depot of several
hundred acres for cotton, stock corrals, and a pen and auction
block used for selling slaves.

April 19   "*Nothing of note.*"

April 20   "*cotton comin down the river.*"

April 21   "*captured from the rebels.*"

April 22   "*never pay the depot full.*"

The 4th Massachusetts returned to Brashear City to draw
guard duty; however, the majority of Banks' troops continued
north to Opelousas, Louisiana. Federal gunboats continued
up the Atchafalaya River to the Red River culminating in
Banks' plan to bypass Port Hudson and strike at the Red River
Confederate supply line.

Unfortunately, Union officers seemed unable to control
their troops on the march to Opelousas, and the countryside

was destroyed. Stragglers stole and burned homes despite orders to the contrary. Dargan's entries for this period refer to Louisiana rum, a mixture of creosote and benzene, heartily consumed by the Union troops. It would be difficult to control an army fired with this mixture! The cotton referred to by the author of the diary was "legal" plunder. By the end of April approximately $10 million worth of private property was confiscated by the Federal army. The cotton "comin' down" river was captured cotton from numerous plantations. His comment of April 22, "never pay," may refer to the fact that the troops had not received any pay since arriving in Louisiana. It could also be interpreted that he was aware that the cotton was confiscated without payment to the plantation owners.

April 27   *"The band played for a funeral a Sgt of the 114 regement."*

April 30   *"paymaster came   paid one company that night."*

The funeral was for a member of the 114th New York Regiment. Dargan's diary entry for the twenty-seventh does not mention the funeral, but states Dr. James Waldock, the surgeon for the 4th Massachusetts, was arrested for straggling with his ambulance corps near Franklin during the Fort Bisland engagement.[6]

Since this is the first time the author of the diary mentions being paid, it may, indeed, be the first time since arriving in Louisiana. The regiment was probably paid before they left camp in December 1862, but not after that. The diarist later states that the April payment was his salary up to March 1, 1863, which would have marginally met the army regulation that, "Payment in arrears would at no time exceed two months." Regulations also called for a $12^{1}/_{2}¢$ deduction per month from enlisted men's pay to support the "Soldiers' Home."[7]

Chapter VI

May 1863
Confiscated Goods and Slaves

May would be a relatively quiet month for the 4th Massachusetts as the unit remained at Brashear City operating as the rear guard. General Banks, however, was far from finished with his expedition to the Red River.

May 1 *"paid the regement of our company   all comps* [companies] *to the first of March."*

May 2 *"Cotton still comin down   Shuger* [sugar] *and molases."*

May 3 *"Sunday service in the fornoon   confictecated property   3 hundred horse and mules come in this week   The city is full of all kinds of confistecated."*

May 4 *"The steem boats keep comin in with cotton."*

Obviously he is amazed by the material and animals that appear daily, all now the property of the U.S. government. The citizens of southern Louisiana were also overwhelmed by the loss of almost all of their possessions.

By early May nearly 20,000 head of animals—horses, mules, and cattle—had been sent south to Brashear City.[1] The Confederate salt supply from mines at Avery Island had been destroyed and hundreds of pounds of salt poured into the depot along with cotton, sugar, and molasses. One other confiscated "commodity" was thousands of Negro slaves no longer officially subservient to plantation owners. These slaves followed the Federal troops, and many of them became soldiers in the Union army or were put to work by the army. Unfortunately, the women, children, old and infirmed would not find life much better.

> ***May 5***   *"The wether is hot   five soldgers lived [?] to pay   I sent my pay home and a letter receved from my wife an papers."*

I believe he means "lined" to pay. The regiment was paid by company with a company officer in attendance to verify daily muster roll entries and appropriate remuneration. That meant the men had to line up and wait their turn. The five men the diarist refers to may have been on detached duty when the paymaster paid out on May 1. Although it was hot and many men died due to disease and lack of sanitation, it is difficult to believe that only five soldiers lived to be paid on May 5. His previous diary entries indicate the paymaster arrived in camp April 30, 1863, and the pay process was undoubtedly delayed since men were deployed at several locations.

> ***May 8***   *"I wrote a letter to my wife."*

> ***May 9***   *"The wether is cold   a suden change   it has been very could* [cold]   *at nights but plesent day   The men hold arguments about the expiren* [expiration] *of ther nine months is up   grate Jaren* [great jawing, a slang term for much talking].*"*

These men were bored. It was hot, then cold; the mosquitoes were terrible, and the food inedible. The excitement of huge amounts of confiscated goods that arrived daily had worn off, and the enemy within the confines of Brashear City was not a threat. The new topic of discussion was the number of days required on active duty to complete their nine-month enlistment. In late June and early July, the men's understanding of a nine-month enlistment would lead to a mutiny in the 4th Massachusetts Infantry Regiment.

The 4th was not the only nine-month unit under General Banks, and the officers of these regiments must have made him aware of the fact that the interpretation of nine-month service was causing much discontent. This began a series of communiqués between Banks and Washington for clarification. Banks requested General in Chief Henry W. Halleck, to advise him on what constituted nine-month service. The men of the regiments thought that their length of service had been determined upon the formation of each individual company. For most men that would have been sometime in September of 1862. The governor of Massachusetts stated his position that nine-month service expired on the date that the last Massachusetts company was formed in the regiment. Under this definition there could easily have been a 30- to 45-day extension in some of the companies' committed time. Banks had a total of 22 regiments enlisted for nine months, and he needed to have an answer from Washington.[2]

General Halleck replied that the question had been referred to the adjutant general for clarification. The adjutant general's office supported the governor of Massachusetts determining the service date expired when the last company was formed in the regiment. That settled the question but left a lot of unhappy, bitter men in Louisiana.

May 9   *"News came that Alexander* [Alexandria] *was taken."*

General Banks had maneuvered his army deeper into the bayou country to advance upon Alexandria, located north on the Red River. Commodore David Porter, in the same time frame, was pushing up the Red River from the east and occupied Alexandria on May 7, just a few hours before General Banks and his troops arrived overland. Confederate General Taylor, with his severely outnumbered troops, had been able to offer only limited resistance, but he was drawing Banks deeper into Louisiana and farther away from Port Hudson.

The Confederate command watched with eager anticipation. Port Hudson was not threatened, and General Banks was not supporting Grant at Vicksburg, thus enabling the beleaguered Confederates to hold their two most important fortifications on the Mississippi River—Port Hudson and Vicksburg.

Washington was watching too but not with the enthusiasm of the Confederates. General in Chief Halleck corresponded with General Banks on May 19, 1863:

Headquarters of the Army

Washington, D. C., May 19, 1863

Major-General Banks,

New Orleans, La.:

GENERAL: I learn from the newspapers that you are in possession of Alexandria, and General Grant of Jackson. This may be well enough so far, but these operations are too eccentric to be pursued. I must again urge that you co-operate as soon as possible with General Grant east of the Mississippi. Your forces must be united at the earliest possible moment. Otherwise the enemy will concentrate on Grant and crush him. Do all you can to prevent this. I have no troops to reinforce him. Both Burnside and Rosecrans are calling loudly for re-enforcements. I have none to give either. I have strongly urged the Navy Department to send the monitors to the Mississippi River, but I am answered that they can do nothing against Vicksburg and Port Hudson.

We shall watch with the greatest anxiety the movements of yourself and General Grant. I have urged him to keep his forces concentrated as much as possible, and not to move east till he gets control of the Mississippi River.

Very respectfully, your obedient servant,

H. W. Halleck

General-in-Chief[3]

The message from Washington was very clear, but again on May 23, 1863, General Halleck advised Banks to get on with the business of Port Hudson. Halleck restated that the opening of the Mississippi River was the first priority and if Banks did not get into serious trouble maneuvering in the back country of Louisiana, it would be due to the enemy failing to seize the opportunity. Another communiqué on May 25 from General Halleck was equally as caustic, as Banks began moving toward Port Hudson.

May 10   *"Sunday   beautyful day   our baggage come up from Algears Servis* [service] *Col Colly* [Colby] *officeated for Chaplin."*

May 11   *"Capten Merrill came from Algears   the recyqusation* [requisition] *when* [went] *in for transportation for Company B."*

Evidently Merrill, captain of Company B, had been in Algiers on detached duty during the Fort Bisland affair. The requisition he filed may have been for the anticipated Union troop movement toward Port Hudson at the end of May.

May 12   *"General Emerry come hear at night."*

May 14   *"The officers had a meeting at Col. Walkers headquarters."*

May 15   *"Nothing of importance."*

May 16   *"260 counter bands* [contrabands] *come down the river to day for the Nigor Brigade."*

The term *contraband* applied to fugitive slaves and was originated by General Benjamin Butler. He referred to them at Fort Monroe, Virginia, as "contrabands of war." The term became part of the Civil War vocabulary and was used by troops and civilians.

May 17   *"Nothing."*

May 19 *"receved a letter from my wife   sent one the same day and three papers."*

May 20 *"our company whent up the river on an excurtion* [excursion] *There was a horne pike cout* [caught] *in the Bayou 63 pounds."*

May 22 *"our company got 10 men wounded on the Louisanner Bell below Washington. Captain Alexander of the boat was killed by the rebels*

Enoch Bradshaw in the back

Thomas Burtler [Butler] *five places*

Shepard [Charles Shaw] *in fore places*

Thomas Wells [Willis] *in both legs*

Wiren [Warren] *Sargent in mouth and head*

Joseph Morgan in the arm

Thimothy Clores [Timothy Cleary] *in side*

C [Thomas] *Butler scrach on the fase* [face]

D [Daniel] *Kiley scrach in side."*

May 23 *"The men was moved to the hospital and doing well."*

It is difficult to determine whether the diarist was aboard the *Louisiana Belle* as part of the expedition. His identification of the wounded men was correct except that he listed Butler twice. He would have known these men well, having been with them since the fall of 1862.

Captain Merrill's report of the incident, written on May 23, explains the entire episode. On May 20, Merrill reported to the *Louisiana Belle* with 50 men from Company B to act as guard aboard ship. The *Louisiana Belle* was en route north to Washington to load plundered cotton. By dawn of the twenty-second, the ship was full and started its return trip down the Bayou Courtableau and was attacked by guerrillas stationed along the banks of the bayou. Captain Alexander, commander of the ship, was killed and a ship's pilot, two deckhands, and the men of Company B were wounded. The main pilot for the ship was able to steer the *Belle* down the bayou and bring her to safety. Captain Merrill estimated there were at least 30 guerrillas in the attack, all in civilian clothes. Merrill claimed 10 men of Company B were wounded. The diarist listed nine men (one listed twice), and the 4th Massachusetts Infantry records show eight.[4]

The dispersion of all confiscated goods was the responsibility of the U.S. government. However, many private individuals made enormous profits on cotton and sugar siphoned from the government warehouses. Some of this black market cotton undoubtedly found its way to the very mills in New England, where many of the men of the 4th Massachusetts had previously labored. Even Colonel Henry Walker from Lawrence, Massachusetts, was not above suspicion for being involved in illegal trade.

May 25 *"a large wagon train come down the Turnpike road from round Washington   5 miles long   was attacked near Franklin by rebels   They was escorted by the 110 New York 114 N. Y. 41 Mass and 90 New York   The rebels turned back."*

This train included some 3,500 animals and 5,000 contraband.

May 27 *"receved a letter from my wife dated the 10."*

May 30 *"we left Brasher City for New Orleans   we arrived at 11 o clock."*

Until this point the diary had been written in ink. From May 30, through the last entry, it is in pencil and very hard to read. Pen and ink were difficult to obtain. Once spent or lost, the soldier wrote with whatever he could find.

The authors of many Civil War letters frequently noted that they had not been able to secure paper or a writing instrument, even in the Union hospitals in Washington. When the 4th Massachusetts departed from Brashear City they left behind personal baggage under guard of men from several units. It may be that the author of the diary decided to leave behind his precious pen and ink since there would have been no doubt in his mind that the assault on Port Hudson was imminent.

May 31 *"It set sail at 10 o clock in the morning to Port Hudson   landed at Spring Field landing 5 miles below Port Hudson."*

Not all of the 4th Massachusetts sailed on the ship that Dargan referred to as an old boat named the *Sallie Robinson,* previously used for goods transport on the Red River. All 10 companies left a contingent on detached guard duty at Brashear City. It appears at least a quarter of Company B did not go to Port Hudson. Dargen states the regiment mustered only 460 men.[5]

General Banks was finally advancing on Port Hudson. Troop movement from Alexandria and Baton Rouge had begun in the latter part of May, and the 4th Massachusetts would be joining the Federal attack force already in place. General Banks estimated his total attack force to be less than 13,000 men. This was a very conservative estimate.

While the 4th was sailing from New Orleans, General Banks made an unsuccessful attack on Port Hudson. The Confederates had held, and Federal losses were 293 killed, 1,549 wounded. A considerable portion of the afternoon of May 28 was consumed by dispatches between General Banks and the Confederate commander of Port Hudson, General Franklin Gardner, to attempt to arrange a cease-fire in order to remove the dead and wounded from the battlefield. By

May 31, Banks requested all Negro troops remaining in New Orleans to be sent to Port Hudson, with or without arms. His request for additional troops from General Grant at Vicksburg was refused.

Chapter VII

June 1863
Death and Mutiny

June would be a month filled with more bloodshed and discomfort than the men of the 4th Massachusetts had previously experienced. This was the final push against Port Hudson, which had been delayed by General Banks since the regiment arrived in Louisiana.

Between June 5 and June 30 the diary entries are illegible. The pencil has worn off, there are water stains, and some pages are possibly missing. The unintelligible portions of the diary can be reconstructed by examining several other sources, including daily reports in the *Official Records* and Dargan's diary.

Port Hudson was heavily fortified by the Confederates since they had the time and the opportunity to prepare while General Banks dragged his feet in the bayous to the west. The Confederates were positioned on a bend of the Mississippi River, where the bluffs fell steeply to the riverbank.

The strategic weak spot was the area behind the Confederate fort to the east, north, and south. If the fort was encircled by Federal troops, there would be no escape. This fortification was dependent on land and river supply lines, with the latter already in jeopardy. If both lines were severed, survival would be impossible.

Confederate General Joseph E. Johnston sent a message to General Gardner on May 21, 1863, which essentially stated: Evacuate! The message was received too late for Gardner to act. Gardner decided to hold his position and made a request to Johnston for troop reinforcement. Gardner was a brave man, who supported the Confederate cause until the bitter end.[1] Gardner was literally encircled by Grant to his north, moving on Vicksburg, Banks on the east and south, and Farragut and his gunboats on the Mississippi to his rear. In addition, Gardner's troops were plagued with disease, and lack of proper rations forced them to eat mules, rats, and whatever else crawled into the trenches. In a month or two his fortification would have collapsed due to starvation. Despite all of these obstacles, he was still a threat to the Mississippi corridor in June 1863.

Banks needed to aggressively attack in order to prove himself as a stalwart general. It was important for him personally to hand Washington a victory since his political aspirations would be enhanced by an outstanding military career.

Gardner had at least 20 heavy guns mounted on the bluffs to harass the Union navy, and four large forts placed at strategic locations around Port Hudson proper. The town itself was nothing more than a small shipping village with very few houses, a handful of stores, and a church. The terrain around the port was difficult to traverse because of the deep ravines, swamps, and heavy forest. All these factors were in Gardner's favor, but Banks had the manpower and supply lines. Union forces in front of Port Hudson greatly outnumbered the Confederates.[2] Gardner's troop strength was estimated to be between five and six thousand men.[3]

Bank's first assault on May 27 had proven disastrous and was an indication of how much resistance there was at Port Hudson.

The first diary entry for June was written at Port Hudson.

June 2 *"lay before the fort in a wood at night   we was shelled at night by the rebels."*

June 4 *"hevey firing on both sides at right   began again that night   the regement was ordered up to the front of the enemany brest works as sharps [sharpshooters]."*

June 5 *"I whent to the rifle pit and was fired on by the rebels   the ball goin [going] past my head   five mortars come to our left at night."*

On June 1 the temperature was 110 degrees in the shade. Men were passing out from sunstroke and water was hard to find. The 4th Massachusetts was in the vicinity of Plains Store, slightly north of Port Hudson, where there was ample evidence of the struggle on May 27. The countryside was destroyed and several freshly dug graves were apparent in the scorched fields. The 12th Maine, 13th Connecticut, and the 4th Massachusetts were put to work digging trenches for cover and assumed picket duty.

The artillery of the Union army posed a deadly threat to the occupants of Port Hudson. Before the siege ended, the Federals could boast of having three guns for every Confederate cannon. Enterprising measures were utilized to protect what guns the Confederates had left; guns were placed in pits when they were not in use to protect them from Union rounds. Eventually the supply of ammunition for the Confederate guns was exhausted, and the loads became any kind of scrap metal they could scrounge. Although superior in number, the Union artillery needed to be moved across ravines and open fields to be effective at optimum range locations. Elaborate infiltration measures were developed by using infantry in trenches to provide fire coverage until the guns were in optimal position.

Union troops used bales of cotton to build temporary fortification lines, as contrabands dug trenches and rifle pits. The spade and shovel played almost as important a role in the siege as did the rifle. If the trenches were deep enough, Confederate rifle fire was ineffective against the advancing Union line. Union troops soon learned not to raise their heads above the trench line, and a hat raised on a bayonet brought a fusillade of fire. Sharpshooters, on both sides, were a constant menace. Confederates were particularly good at climbing tall trees, concealing themselves, and picking off Union men at ranges sometimes approaching three-quarters of a mile. Many of these Alabama, Mississippi, and Arkansas boys had experience as squirrel hunters since the time they were old enough to carry guns.

On June 5, 1863, Banks issued orders to General Halbert E. Paine to launch an expedition to Clinton, northeast of Port Hudson, to drive the enemy from that general area. Since Clinton was located to the rear of Banks' headquarters, he needed to secure the entire perimeter. The raid did drive the Confederates out of the Clinton countryside, but they continued to harass the Federals at other locations.[4]

Each day brought constant skirmishing along the Port Hudson line, but Dargan's diary indicates that the 4th Massachusetts was not always engaged. The 4th manned picket duty, spent a lot of time resting to escape the heat, and enjoyed an occasional whiskey ration. Union troops complained that they should not be the ones to fill sandbags, roll out cotton bales for gunfire protection, or dig trenches—that type of work was for the contrabands.

The spades were kept busy digging trenches and roads were constructed for artillery wagons, while the Confederate sharpshooters made all the work very risky. The 4th Massachusetts and other troops were instructed in the use of hand grenades by General Paine, an omen of what was about to occur. Under a flag of truce to recover the dead and wounded, the Rebels and the Yankees conversed, traded hardtack and newspapers, and bantered back and forth. It could hardly be called a gentlemen's war, but it did have its respites from killing.

By mid-month it was obvious that this "give and take" warfare could not continue. The Federals needed to push hard to bring Port Hudson to its knees. Grant was engaged in Vicksburg and making inroads, while Washington, and indeed the entire North, watched. General Halleck wrote Banks to inquire about his moving on Port Hudson, because Halleck thought Banks was supposed to be supporting Grant at Vicksburg. Halleck stated he could not believe the reports were true. Two months before, Halleck had been sending messages to Banks telling him to get out of the bayou country, cooperate with Grant, and take Port Hudson. Banks certainly had not exhibited much strategic ability or assertive leadership, but he thought he was doing what Washington wanted. Although communication channels were slow, these two men were obviously not making any great effort to keep each other informed.[5]

On June 4, Banks replied to Halleck that he would be able to reduce Port Hudson within a week, despite his recent unproductive maneuvers in the bayou country. Upon his arrival at Port Hudson on May 25, Banks thought he would receive support from General Grant. He did not, and now Banks was engaged in a major conflict alone. The Confederates were back in the bayou country threatening the area he recently conquered, which could lead to the loss of New Orleans. If Banks abandoned Port Hudson to support Grant, the Confederates would be free to move on the lower Mississippi. Banks' decision-making process was constantly impacted by his tendency to underestimate his troop strength and to overestimate Confederate strength. In any case, he was committed to taking Port Hudson.

On June 13 the Federals made an all-out artillery assault and ended the barrage with a flag of truce. General Banks forwarded a letter to General Gardner at Port Hudson requesting immediate surrender to avoid further bloodshed. Gardner replied that his duty was to defend his position and would not surrender.[6] Admiral Farragut prepared his fleet to support Banks in the bombardment of Port Hudson and thus began a bloody battle.

Late in the afternoon of June 13, the 4th Massachusetts was mustered and listened to an address from Banks. The Federals would attack Port Hudson again tomorrow. The lead assault regiments were to be the nine-month units including the 4th. Banks issued orders on June 11, in anticipation of Gardner's refusal to surrender, that stated very clearly that the nine-month units would lead the advance attack. Those units had not seen a great deal of action in their short time in the military, which may have motivated Banks to use them in the front. It was a way to take the pressure off those men who enlisted for three years and had already seen their share of action. Banks and his staff must have realized they had a ticking time bomb that still prevailed among the troops of the nine-month units concerning the question of the actual days a nine-month man had to serve. The regiments were provided a generous whiskey ration to help take their minds off what daylight would bring.

At 2 A.M. on June 14, two companies of the 4th Massachusetts were rallied with another issue of whiskey and rations. The forward order came at about dawn, and the troops advanced through heavy fog towards the fort. Many men were killed, maimed, or wounded. Orders were passed to lie down. General Paine, in an attempt to gain ground, rose to lead the troops and was hit by rifle fire. He suffered a broken leg and left the troops with no definitive leadership. Dargan was hit in the head and retired to the rear for medical attention. The attack lost all coordination and direction with few men reaching the Confederate parapets. Those who succeeded were killed, wounded, or captured. The rest of the day continued in an endless bloodbath with troops in the wrong location and floundering due to the lack of direction. When darkness came and the action ceased, there were some 1,800 casualties to be added to the Union reports, and the Confederates still held Port Hudson having lost only 47 men.

According to Dargan, Joseph H. Gould, the assistant surgeon of the 4th Massachusetts, remained at the front lines to administer to the wounded. The wounded were separated based on the severity of their wounds; those with mortal wounds were laid aside, while those who had a chance to survive were lined up for medical treatment. Amputations at the general hospital to the rear were numerous. Dargan's diary states the 4th Massachusetts had 70 men killed, wounded, or missing.[7] The *Official Records* state that the actual number of men from the 4th Massachusetts who were killed or wounded at Port Hudson was 68, indicating that Dargan's estimate was very close to the actual number.[8] The regiment had been unfortunate enough to be in the lead assault, so their chances for injury were magnified. On subsequent days there were skirmishes at Port Hudson but no fatalities and only one wounding among the 4th Massachusetts.

Although the 4th Massachusetts still had three weeks ahead of them at Port Hudson, they would be limited to mostly picket and guard duty. The regiment's performance had not been stellar on the fourteenth. Apparently not every man threw his heart and soul into the attack due to the gnawing question of the nine-month service expiration date. Banks may have thought that he had clarified the point earlier, but the troops did not accept the official government position. Many men had enlisted during the first part of September 1862, meaning that they had served their nine months by the end of May 1863. On June 18, General Banks reported to Halleck that one reason he was stalled in front of Port Hudson was because of the refusal of his nine-month regiments to do perilous duty. A letter from General Grover specifically cites the 4th Massachusetts as acting in a cowardly manner. Halleck suggested that the dissenters be formed into an attack column with artillery to their rear to be fired at the first indication of wavering.[9]

The attack day of June 14, 1863, was one of high probability of death or wounding. Out of this time of grim reality came one shining star associated with the 4th Massachusetts. First Sergeant George M. Lovering, Company I, was awarded the Medal of Honor for his action on June 14. Lovering was a 32-year-old boot maker from East Randolph, Massachusetts, who served in another Civil War unit after the 4th was mustered out in August 1863. The congressional Medal of Honor was authorized March 3, 1863. It was awarded to men for "distinguished gallantry in action outside the line of duty."[10]

The Port Hudson campaign became a siege with both sides attempting to strengthen fortifications. There were still sharpshooters active on both sides, but heat and illness killed more men than those sharp-eyed riflemen located in trees and along ravine edges. The Confederates were without medical supplies, had very little food, and their drinking water was contaminated by the remains of dead men and animals. They could not possibly hold out unless General Johnston sent troops to reinforce their position. That would not happen. The Confederates simply did not have the manpower.

General Banks began planning his third assault as he received news from his staff in New Orleans regarding Rebel troop movement to the south and west. The Port Hudson affair needed to come to a close in order for Federal troops to be dispersed to control Confederate action in the bayou country. The trouble began around mid-June as Confederates pushed down the Mississippi below Baton Rouge, skirmished at Plaquemine taking Union prisoners, and moved on to

Lafourche Crossing on the Great Western Railroad, which placed them between New Orleans and Brashear City.

Colonel Albert Stickney of the 47th Massachusetts Infantry was in command of the area. A wire from General Emory in New Orleans alerted Stickney to the danger in the area. Stickney left Brashear City to advance to Lafourche Crossing, leaving Major Robert C. Anthony of the 2nd Rhode Island Cavalry in charge of defenses at Brashear City. Stickney subsequently encountered the Rebels, and a skirmish occurred with loss of life on both sides. In the interim the Confederates had commandeered skiffs and boats of all types, crossed Grand Lake, and approached the rear of Brashear City. Unaware of this, the Union troops were watching their front where Rebels were shelling Berwick City. Major Anthony had been warned of possible attack around June 20, but absolutely no defensive preparations had been made, and on June 23, 1863, the Confederates captured Brashear City from the rear.[11]

The military stores and personal regimental material were to have been removed from Brashear City in late May, but these orders were never executed. Consequently, all of the 4th Massachusetts Infantry Regiment's equipment and records were captured and destroyed as well as those of several other regiments. All personal possessions left behind by the men fighting at Port Hudson were gone. Although figures differ, basically 325 Confederates captured the city, with only 3 killed and 18 wounded. They took approximately 1,200 Union prisoners, many of whom were convalescents, 11 cannon, 2,500 Enfield and Burnside rifles, 2,000 Negroes, and quartermaster commissary stores.

On June 27, things at Port Hudson went from bad to worse for the 4th Massachusetts. There was mutiny in the regiment; men refused to report for duty and were sent to General Banks, and the regimental flag was confiscated. The men were told that they had to return to duty on June 30; if not, the entire regiment would be incarcerated for the duration of the war. One hundred thirty-nine enlisted men and five commissioned officers were arrested.

The diary resumes at the end of June.

June 30   *"The 130 men was taken to General Glovers* [Grover's] *headquarters then to Banks   our men returned to duty."*

At Grover's headquarters the officers and noncommissioned officers surrendered their side arms, and the insignia was removed from each of their uniforms. The men were marched off to Banks' headquarters and confined to log cabins under guard of the 31st Massachusetts. The men who returned to duty on June 30 were the remaining 4th Massachusetts troops who did not mutiny or decided to obey General Banks' order to return to duty.

Records in Lawrence, Massachusetts, indicate that Company B did not become involved in the mutiny, but 21 members of Company H were arrested by General Grover. The remainder of the one hundred plus mutineers were from Company A (including officers), Company C, Company D (Corporal Dargan was not involved), Company E, Company G, (including officers), and Company K. Interestingly, every man in Company H who joined the mutiny had enlisted in late August or very early September 1862. As far as they were concerned, their nine-month enlistment had expired, a common sentiment also expressed by the men in the other companies. The mutineers were incarcerated for over two months in Louisiana.

Chapter VIII

July 1863
Port Hudson Falls

The Union field hospitals were overflowing, so many of the wounded were put into wagons to be taken to Springfield Landing where they were placed on steamers bound for Baton Rouge. The trip from the battlefield to Springfield Landing took almost 12 hours, jolting over rough roads in unbearably hot and humid weather. Some of the soldiers did not survive that ride.

July 1 *"the first the rebels got two guns in opperation our guns could not get at them   the rebels keep aiming in our rear and keep anuning [annoying] us all the time   we had to go and fight then."*

"the men meet to heer General Banks make a speach   the men do not cheer him   they gave a small clap at the finish   He told them that he would have the Stars and Stripes flying in Port Hudson on the morning of the forth of July."

July 3 *"The rebels killed too of our nigors and wounded three privets and one Lutenant and we gave then all they wanted."*

The wounded, who were transported to Springfield Landing in order to be subsequently evacuated, found themselves in the middle of enemy action on July 2. Confederate cavalry surprised pickets posted along the road, burnt supplies, and caused general havoc. The disorganization and panic were attributed to inexperienced Negro troops guarding the area, contraband concentration, and, most of all, picket negligence. A recommendation was made to General Banks to reposition Federal troops and to relocate contraband not involved in work parties to the New Orleans area. Evidently, there were large numbers of women, children, and older men unable to perform heavy duties who were simply following the Union army.[1]

In New Orleans, on July 3, a curfew was established by General Emory, commander of Federal defenses in that city. No more than a group of three people were allowed to assemble on the streets, and all shops were to be closed at 9 P.M. Emory was very nervous about being able to hold New Orleans if a Confederate force attacked. On the Fourth of July he wrote to General Halleck in Washington requesting reinforcements because he was convinced that the Rebels were approaching with a force of 15,000 men.

There was continued unrest among the Union troops in front of Port Hudson. They were tired, riddled with physical ailments, and suspicious of Banks' ability to take the fort. The nine-month enlistment controversy was temporarily under control due to the arrest of the mutinous members of the 4th Massachusetts, but dissension still simmered. Some officers were put under arrest for making disparaging statements about the futility of the campaign. The siege continued with daily loss of life, constant trenching edging closer to the Confederate lines, engineers placing explosive charges and limited storming maneuvers.

July 4 *"The men all expect to take the fort today but they was nothing about it   That made three times Banks had deceved the men in regards the day we should take the fort and the men have very little faith in him with the bad mangemnt of the attack on the fort and the way he has deceved them time and again*

The 4th of July ended as miserble as it began   About fore o'clock a storm arose and then turned into the hevest rain I ever saw My clothes was whet and I had to sleep in them."

"This makes 15 days that I have had the disentery and I am very week and do not mend easy."

July 5   *"Hevy firing at bouth sides."*

July 6   *"our men is close to the enemys brest works   Our men gave them some tobaco throwen it over the brest works Throwen letters to one another."*

Two days before the men exchanged articles across the lines in Louisiana, their fellow comrades in arms suffered great losses at Gettysburg. General Lee was retreating back to Virginia after fighting one of the most controversial battles of the Civil War. The troops were unaware that General Grant had conquered Vicksburg on the same day. It was a very black day for the Confederacy, but, even so, the Civil War would grind on until the spring of 1865.

July 7   *"News came heer that Vixburge was taken at eight o'clock   our generals sent news all round to the camps great cheers was given all round   The rebels wonderd what was the matter   Our men hollered and tould them   they did not like it   our regement has been right up to the enemys brest works too days and too nights with no sleep."*

July 8   *"I woke up this morning after 9 dredful nights firing and the rebels have the flag of truce up   we whent to se the cause   they was about to surender if we cold [could] ashure them that Vexburge was taken   so we sent in the dispach   thay then made arangments to surender at 1 o'clock   Things did not get setld [settled] till afternoon   our boys was with the rebels all day talking and trading small things and troops got orders to march in the fort at 5   This night we got some bad news   the rebels had took posesion of Brasher city   all our* *cloths* [clothes] *my loss was from sixty to seventy dollars   There was 127 prisoners in our companies   Ther was 19 in Ingham* [Colonel Ingraham] *unit   raged* [ragged] *and dirty and no change and dont now* [know] *where I shall get any and still no signs for home."*

The fighting was over for the 4th Massachusetts Infantry Regiment, but they had lost all of their personal possessions that they thought were safe in Brashear City. The diary's author indicates despondency with his statement, "...still no signs for home." That had to be first and foremost on all of their minds, and they probably thought they would be sent home immediately. Unfortunately, these men would not be discharged until the end of August.

On July 7, Admiral Farragut contacted General Banks offering to approach Port Hudson under a flag of truce to demand surrender of the fort. Farragut knew, of course, that Vicksburg had fallen and the fort was likely to surrender based on that news. He felt Gardner would be more willing to surrender to the navy "on account of the negro question." Farragut reasoned that the Confederates would be reluctant to surrender to an army utilizing Negro troops. Banks declined. This had been his ground battle, and the surrender was to be his despite the support of the Union navy.[2]

During the day of the seventh, General Gardner requested official acknowledgment of Vicksburg's surrender, and if true, he would agree to the cessation of hostilities. Banks provided the official notification, rejected Gardner's cessation of hostilities, but requested his generals stop military action. By pressing for proof of Vicksburg's collapse and then delaying the time for actual surrender, Gardner provided an opportunity for many of his men to escape before the Federals occupied the fort. Gardner surrendered on July 8 and requested a delegation of officers to discuss surrender terms. An unconditional surrender was signed at 2 P.M., and it stated that the

Union occupation force would enter the fort at 5 P.M. Banks lost no time in notifying Grant that Port Hudson had fallen, and he would take formal possession at 7 A.M. on July 9.

July 9 "*Our regement whent in to the fort to do garison duty it was an awful looking place inside the right front and left was not as strong as our soldgers thought it was we marched to the front to the water batterys the rebels was at that part of the fort and we was to gard them There was six thousand 5 hundred* [men] *There was 42 peces of cannon 5 hundred horse and mules and 8 thousand 6 hundred stand of small arms and a fair quanity of americhon* [ammunition] *and other things 10 of our boys begang to trade with the rebels it would last from morning till the last thing at night our boys got lots of cloths for nothing most new our men begang to trade ther ruber blankts for the white ones and comfrit* [?] *blanet* [blanket].*"*

General Banks ordered seven of his nine-month regiments, including the 4th Massachusetts, into Port Hudson on July 9 for garrison guard duty. The figures for captured men and equipment listed in the diary are very close to actual count expressed in the *Official Records*. General Banks and General Halleck filed reports containing differing numbers than General Gardner, who reported a smaller number of arms surrendered.[3]

July 11 "*The prisoners are getting ther perrole today.*"

The process of paroling the Confederate prisoners began on July 11, 1863. Parole was a system used for dealing with large numbers of captured men who the conquering force could not possibly transport to prisons or guard for any long period of time. The number of men captured frequently outnumbered the troops who captured them. This was true at Brashear City when the Confederates overran the Federal garrison. The terms of a parole required a prisoner to give his word not to return to active duty until he was exchanged for enemy captives of equal rank. It was a gentlemen's agreement and an antiquated system that was severely restricted during the last two years of the Civil War.

All enlisted men, noncommissioned officers, and Confederate employees captured at the fort signed a parole form and were released with a supply of rations. Parole records reveal that almost six thousand men went through this process at Port Hudson.

Approximately 450 officers, who were taken as prisoners, were not paroled, but were kept as prisoners of war and were housed under guard in New Orleans. Eventually, at least half of the men were sent to Northern prison camps while several managed to escape.

July 12 *"General Banks brought his headquarters in side the fort today. General andrew is the commander of Port Hudson The 50 band [50th Massachusetts] come up to day to prade at General Banks and Andrews headquarters Col Colley [Colby] whent after [?] after Colley [Colby] telling the regement to go ther and [?] all things belonging to the regement Col Walker come up to the regement late at night no one looked at him as he pased in."*

July 13 *"the rebels ar goin away as they get perroled they begin too look [?] Alex Warner come up to day with some prisoners from New Orleans he brout me a good drink of wiskey first for six weeks."*

July 14 *"the prisoners mostly all gone to day."*

The General Andrews referred to in the diary is General Leonard Andrews, who served as Banks' chief of staff at Port Hudson. By July 15, all enlisted Confederate soldiers except the sick and wounded who could not be moved were paroled and dispersed. The Confederate surgeon in charge of the Rebel hospital in Clinton requested that invalids from Port Hudson be sent to his hospital. The request was denied based upon the conditions of the patients and the fact that medical supplies were more readily available at Port Hudson. At least one Confederate surgeon remained at the fort to aid the Union doctors.

July 16   *"nothing of importance."*

July 17   *"nothing of importance."*

On July 17, the 4th Massachusetts Infantry Regiment moved to a new campsite outside the fort. Those on garrison guard duty remained within the fort and on the ramparts. Most of the unit's men were reunited at the camp except for those still in hospitals and at paroled locations. This was the first attempt to organize the regiment in preparation for the trip home to Massachusetts.

July 18   *"no signs for home."*

The diary entries dated between July 16 and July 20 indicate that the diarist was thinking mostly about going home.

July 20   *"no signs for home."*

July 22   *"The 52 Mass started for home."*

July 23   *"24 Maine started for home up river."*

General Charles P. Stone, who was in charge of administrative affairs at Port Hudson, reported on July 20 that he had selected the 52nd Maine as the first unit to be sent home due to their enthusiasm to serve with no instances of insubordination. Although not written as orders, it became obvious that the poor-performance regiments would be the last ones to be sent North.[4] One company of the 50th Massachusetts refused to do guard duty, so they were arrested. General Stone reported that dysentery and measles were sweeping his command resulting in a very high mortality rate, which added to the men's desire to go home.

July 24 *"Our boys come up that was taken prisoner at Ship Island and joined the regement at Port Hudson."*

This is the last entry in the diary. Succeeding pages are lost. The "our boys" he refers to were the men captured at Brashear City in June, who were paroled and subsequently sent to Ship Island located in the Gulf of Mexico.

Port Hudson became the assembly center for the eventual detachment of the nine-month regiments. The approximately 450 men of the 4th who had fought at Port Hudson were joined by the ill and wounded, paroled ex-prisoners of the Confederates, and those who had been on detached duty. Dargan's diary indicates that the men convening at Port Hudson had to contend with all types of illness, including scurvy, and lived in lice-infested quarters. They drank corn beer, played cards, and argued—anything to pass the time.

With Brashear City back in the hands of the Federals, most of the Union troops, whose enlistment period had not expired, were dispersed from the Port Hudson area to engage the Confederates in southern Louisiana. The war was far from over for them, but for the 4th Massachusetts Infantry Regiment awaiting transportation north, home appeared to be a reality.

Chapter IX
August–September 1863
Goin' Home

Most of the men of the 4th Massachusetts Infantry Regiment boarded the steamer *North America* on August 4 for the first portion of their trip home. Dargan's notes depict a long, unpleasant journey.

All of the ill and wounded were put aboard the ship the night before its scheduled sailing. The men of the 4th Massachusetts Infantry, minus the mutineers, boarded in the early morning. The steamer departed at 7 A.M. to run up the Mississippi River by the Port Hudson bluffs. This was the first time that the men of the 4th had been able to completely see the strategic positioning of Port Hudson. The mouth of the Red River appeared about 3 P.M., and the steamer halted at Natchez for the night.

By midnight, August 5, the troops reached Vicksburg and were allowed on shore while the steamer took on coal. Three men of the 4th died that night and were buried along the river. At 6 P.M. on the seventh, the *North America* continued onward and reached the Arkansas River at about noon on the eighth where two more men were buried in hardtack packing boxes.

On the tenth, the troops reached Memphis where the steamer again took on coal while the men spent time ashore. The early morning hours found the 4th en route to New Madrid,

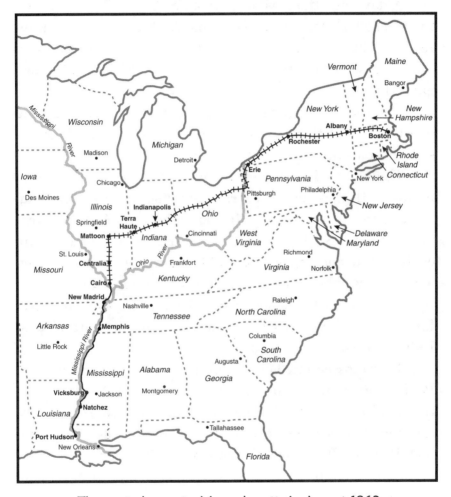

The route home to Massachusetts in August 1863

Drawn by Jim Robinson, Beidel Printing House, Inc.

Missouri, where the ship docked at Island No. 10. This was the site of a Confederate fort captured April 8, 1862, by the Union army on its drive to open up the Mississippi corridor.

A day later the steamer docked at Cairo, Illinois, where the troops boarded baggage cars on the Illinois Central Railroad for the last leg of the trip. They encountered the 35th Massachusetts Infantry Regiment en route to joining their brigade. The men of the 35th inquired about where the colors were for the 4th Regiment. Dargan refers to it as "a killing question," since their flag was still in General Banks' possession in Louisiana.[1]

The railroad transported the men through the rolling plains of Illinois, past Centralia, and south of Springfield, Illinois, to a town named Mattoon where they were transferred to the St. Louis Railroad, arriving at Terre Haute early on the morning of August 14. Indianapolis was reached about 5 P.M. where the Sanitary Commission administered to the needs of the troops.[2] Some men, too sick to travel farther, were removed from the train and hospitalized in Indianapolis.

They crossed into Ohio on August 15 and arrived in Erie, Pennsylvania, about 10 P.M. the following day. They boarded the New York Central Railroad to Rochester, New York, where the men were provided food, soap, and towels. The trip continued through Albany on to Boston, Massachusetts, where they arrived in the afternoon of the seventeenth after a tiring two-week trip. It must have been a touching scene as the men disembarked from the train. Friends and family knew the 4th was "comin' home," so there were happy reunions but also much sadness for those who had no one to greet them. Some families who expected their loved ones to be aboard the train discovered the men were in prison back in Louisiana as a result of the mutiny or did not survive the journey home.

Civil War records enumerating total personnel loss for a unit are not always accurate. This would be compounded in the case of the 4th Massachusetts Infantry Regiment where all regimental records were destroyed at Brashear City. The unit figures provided after the regiment returned to Massachusetts are as follows:

Killed in action—One officer and nineteen enlisted men. Died due to disease—Two officers and one hundred twenty-nine enlisted men.[3]

Dargan states 225 men were lost but most likely that is an inflated figure. Somewhere between his assertion and the reconstruction of company records are the actual figures.[4]

The members of the 4th Massachusetts Infantry Regiment were granted a 10-day furlough and ordered to report to Camp Joe Hooker on August 28 to be mustered out of service. Many of them had been in the army for almost a year. On September 7, 1863, General Banks issued Special Orders No. 223, which made minor arrangements for his troops in Louisiana and released the imprisoned 4th Massachusetts Infantry mutineers. The newly released mutineers were provided provisions, clothing, and transportation to Boston via the Quartermaster Corps. By September 25, 1863, these men had returned to Massachusetts and had received honorable discharges.

General Banks remained in Louisiana to conduct a disastrous campaign in the Red River country. Grant, pushed to the end of his patience, removed Banks from high level command, which ended Banks' political aspirations for the presidency of the United States. He left the army in August 1865 and served as congressman and senator for the state of Massachusetts. On September 1, 1894, Banks died in Waltham, Massachusetts.

General Ulysses S. Grant accepted General Robert E. Lee's surrender in April 1865. Grant served as president of the

United States from 1869 to 1877, though not quite as success-
fully as he managed military campaigns. His administrations
were replete with unethical cabinet members and advisors,
questionable business dealings, bribes, and scandals. Almost
destitute, Grant died from throat cancer on July 23, 1885.

General Gardner remained a prisoner of war until he was
exchanged in August 1864. He then served under Confederate General Richard Taylor for the remainder of the war. He
later returned to Louisiana and his occupation as a planter.
On April 29, 1873, Gardner died at his plantation.

General Johnston took command of the Confederate Army
of the Tennessee in November 1863. Faced with commanding
an army with inadequate supplies and manpower, his strategy was to "hit and run" as Union General William T. Sherman
approached Atlanta. Jefferson Davis demanded offensive action and replaced Johnston. In February 1865, Johnston was
reassigned by General Robert E. Lee to halt Sherman's march
to the sea, which resulted in Johnston's surrender to Sherman
on April 29, 1865. In civilian life he was active in politics and
was appointed the U.S. Commissioner of Railroads in 1885.
On March 21, 1891, Johnston died in Washington, D.C.

The areas where the 4th Massachusetts marched through
mud and swamps no longer resemble the cities of 1863. Many
are now residential suburbs, and urban sprawl has erased
many landmarks. Neither the shoe factories nor the textile
mills still exist in Massachusetts. There is no longer a need
for the occupations of bootmakers, spinners, and bonnet press-
ers in which many of the men of the regiment were employed.
Port Hudson is now a state park commemorating the sacri-
fices made by the men who served there during the Civil
War.

The men returned to civilian life full of goals, dreams,
and memories. Some of them suffered during their remaining
years from injuries and diseases contracted during their year

in the army. For those of the 4th who gave their lives, may
they be remembered in the words of Francis Miles Finch:

> By the flow of the inland river,
> Whence the fleets of iron have fled,
> Where the blades of the grave-grass quiver,
> Asleep are the ranks of the dead;

> Under the sod and the dew,
> Waiting the Judgment Day;
> Under the one, the Blue;
> Under the other, the Gray.[*]

---

[*] First and second verses of *The Blue and the Gray,* a poem written by Francis Miles
Finch, circa 1867.

82

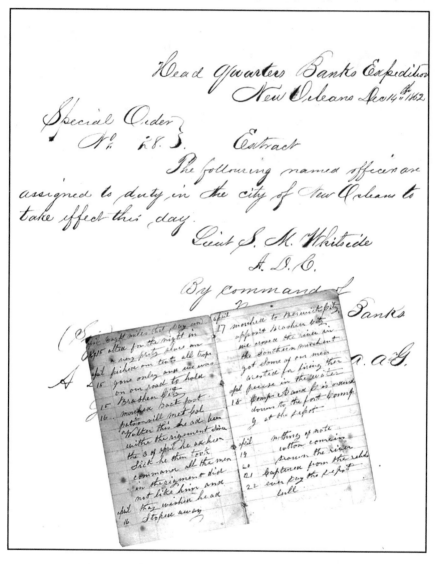

The diary that prompted the publication of this book, and an
original Special Order issued from General Banks' headquarters,
December 14, 1862

Colonel Henry Walker, 4th Massachusetts Infantry

Roger D. Hunt Collection,
U.S. Army Military History Institute,
Carlisle, Pennsylvania

Major Charles F. Howard, 4th Massachusetts Infantry

Massachusetts Commandery Military Order
of the Loyal Legion, and the USAMHI

Regional Quartermaster Lieutenant Thomas J. Lothrop,
4th Massachusetts Infantry

Massachusetts Commandery Military Order
of the Loyal Legion, and the USAMHI

Assistant Surgeon Joseph H. Gould,
4th Massachusetts Infantry

Captain George S. Merrill, Company B, 4th Massachusetts Infantry
Lieutenant John K. Tarbox, Company B, 4th Massachusetts Infantry
Lieutenant Colonel Ebenezer T. Colby, 4th Massachusetts Infantry

Massachusetts Commandery Military Order
of the Loyal Legion, and the USAMHI

Captain John R. Rollins, Company H, 4th Massachusetts Infantry

Massachusetts Commandery Military Order
of the Loyal Legion, and the USAMHI

Lieutenant Albert F. Dow, Company B, 4th Massachusetts Infantry

Massachusetts Commandery Military Order
of the Loyal Legion, and the USAMHI

Postwar photograph of Sergeant Aaron A. Currier,
Company B, 4th Massachusetts Infantry

Robert Cecil Hull, Lawrence Masonic Association,
Lawrence, Massachusetts

Private George E. Harrub, Company E, 4th Massachusetts Infantry

Harrub died on the steamer *North America* while his regiment was being transported home in August 1863.

Private Hiram A. Stearns, Company B, 4th Massachusetts Infantry

Stearns also served in the 6th Massachusetts Infantry and is wearing a hat showing the 6th designation.

Appendix

Roster of the 4th Massachusetts Infantry Regiment— Nine-Month Volunteers

FIELD AND STAFF

Colonel Henry Walker, Quincy; 30 years old; lawyer; commissioned Dec. 6, 1862. Also served as Adjutant, 4th Mass. Infantry for 3-month duty in 1861.

Lieut. Colonel Ebenezer T. Colby, Lawrence; 29 years old; paymaster; commissioned Dec. 6, 1862. Colby was a paymaster at the Pacific Mills textile company in Lawrence and after the war a Custom House inspector in Boston. He died July 24, 1904, survived by his wife, Jennie, and one daughter. Also served in the 4th Mass. Infantry for 3-month duty in 1861.

Major Charles F. Howard, Foxboro; 39 years old; carpenter; commissioned Dec. 6, 1862.

Adjutant Augustus Crocker, Taunton; 22 years old; clerk; commissioned Dec. 15, 1862.

Quartermaster Thomas J. Lothrop, Taunton; 29 years old; lawyer; commissioned Dec. 13, 1862.

Surgeon James Waldock, Roxbury; 39 years old; surgeon; commissioned Dec. 26, 1862. Taken prisoner June 23, 1863, at Brashear City, La.

Assistant Surgeon Edward W. Nortoni, Blandford; 32 years old; surgeon; commissioned Dec. 26, 1862.

Assistant Surgeon Joseph H. Gould, Boston; 33 years old; surgeon; commissioned Dec. 26, 1862.

Chaplain Samuel E. Pierce, Gloucester; 35 years old; minister; commissioned Dec. 26, 1862. Resigned Aug. 25, 1863.

Non-Commissioned Staff

Sergt. Major Franklin Jacobs, Canton; 27 years old; teacher; enlisted Sept. 17, 1862, appointed Sergt. Major, Dec. 6, 1862. Originally Sergt. in Company A.

Quartermaster Sergt. Edwin Barrows, Norton; 29 years old; clerk; enlisted Sept. 19, 1862, appointed Quartermaster Sergt., Dec. 6, 1862. Originally a private in Company F.

Commissary Sergt. Le Baron Goodwin, Duxbury; 26 years old; machinist; enlisted Sept. 22, 1862, appointed Commissary Sergt., Dec. 6, 1862. Originally Sergt. in Company I.

Drum Major Joseph H. Mulhare, Lawrence; 26 years old; mason; enlisted Aug. 28, 1862, appointed Drum Major, Dec. 6, 1862. Originally in Company H.

Principal Music Nelson Mann, Randolph; 29 years old; clerk; enlisted Sept. 17, 1862, appointed Principal Music, Dec. 6, 1862. Originally in Company D.

Hospital Steward Charles W. Howland, Abington; 24 years old; civil engineer; enlisted Sept. 23, 1862, appointed Hospital Steward, Dec. 6, 1862. Originally Sergt. in Company E.

Company A

Captain John Hall, Canton; 44 years old; blacksmith; commissioned Sept. 11, 1862. Wounded June 14, 1863, at Port Hudson, La.

1st Lieut. Ira Drake, Stoughton; 28 years old; bootmaker; commissioned Sept. 11, 1862. Also served in Company A, 4th Mass. Infantry for 3-month duty in 1861.

2d Lieut. Henry U. Morse, Canton; 30 years old; machinist; commissioned Sept. 11, 1862. Taken prisoner June 13, 1863, at Brashear City, La. Also served in Company A, 4th Mass. Infantry for 3-month duty in 1861.

1st Sergt. Jedediah M. Bird, Stoughton; 21 years old; carpenter; enlisted Sept. 17, 1862. Taken prisoner June 23, 1863, at Brashear City, La. Also served in Company A, 4th Mass. Infantry for 3-month duty in 1861.

Sergt. David T. Ward, Stoughton; 35 years old; painter; enlisted Sept. 17, 1862. Appointed Sergt. from Corpl., June 14, 1863. Wounded the same day at Port Hudson, La.

Sergt. Henry Taylor, Canton; 23 years old; machinist; enlisted Sept. 17, 1862. Also served in Company A, 4th Mass. Infantry for 3-month duty in 1861.

Sergt. Charles Taylor, Stoughton; 25 years old; bootmaker; enlisted Sept. 17, 1862. Appointed Sergt. from Corpl., Dec. 6, 1862. Also served in Company A, 4th Mass. Infantry for 3-month duty in 1861.

Sergt. John W. Ayer, Canton; 26 years old; coachman; enlisted Sept. 17, 1862. Died of disease June 5, 1863, at Brashear City, La. Also served in Company A, 4th Mass. Infantry for 3-month duty in 1861.

Sergt. Charles E. Bootman, Canton; 24 years old; painter; enlisted Sept. 17, 1862. Killed June 14, 1863, at Port Hudson, La. Also served in Company A, 4th Mass. Infantry for 3-month duty in 1861.

Corpl. Jerome B. Snow, Canton; 44 years old; laborer; enlisted Sept. 17, 1862. Died of disease July 10, 1863, at New Orleans, La.

Corpl. Henry A. Freeman, Canton; 24 years old; operator; enlisted Sept. 17, 1862. Also served in Company A, 4th Mass. Infantry for 3-month duty in 1861.

Corpl. Elijah A. Morse, Sharon; 21 years old; manufacturer; enlisted Sept. 17, 1862. Taken prisoner June 23, 1863, at Brashear City, La. Also served in Company A, 4th Mass. Infantry for 3-month duty in 1861.

Corpl. George W. Allen, Stoughton; 26 years old; bootmaker; enlisted Sept. 17, 1862.

Corpl. John F. Farnham, Canton; 26 years old; tailor; enlisted Sept. 17, 1862. Taken prisoner June 23, 1863, at Brashear City, La.

Corpl. Charles C. Nichols, Stoughton; 28 years old; carriage trimmer; enlisted Sept. 17, 1862.

Music Warren S. Skinner, Sharon; 16 years old; operator; enlisted Sept. 17, 1862.

Wagoner Charles O. Fuller, Canton; 28 years old; teamster; enlisted Sept. 17, 1862. Died of disease Jan. 28, 1863, at New Orleans, La.

Wagoner William Ford, Canton; 39 years old; blacksmith; enlisted Sept. 17, 1862.

Priv. Gilbert Bell, Stoughton; 39 years old; bootmaker; enlisted Sept. 17, 1862. Taken prisoner June 23, 1863, at Brashear City, La.

Priv. James Berry, Canton; 23 years old; laborer; enlisted Sept. 17, 1862.

Priv. William E. Brewster; Canton, 19 years old; clerk; enlisted Sept. 17, 1862. Died of disease June 3, 1863, at Brashear City, La.

Priv. Edwin A. Briggs, Canton; 18 years old; weaver; enlisted Sept. 17, 1862. Wounded June 14, 1863, at Port Hudson, La.

Priv. Hiram J. Briggs, Canton; 22 years old; weaver; enlisted Sept. 17, 1862.

Priv. Daniel W. Bright, Sharon; 23 years old; farmer; enlisted Sept. 17, 1862. Died of disease May 11, 1863, at Brashear City, La.

Priv. Thomas S. Broadbent, Canton; 43 years old; roll coverer; enlisted Sept. 17, 1862. Taken prisoner June 23, 1863, at Brashear City, La.

Priv. James S. Byrne, Canton; 28 years old; iron heater; enlisted Sept. 17, 1862. Wounded June 14, 1863, at Port Hudson, La.

Priv. John D. Capen, Canton; 20 years old; clerk; enlisted Sept. 17, 1862. Taken prisoner June 23, 1863, at Brashear City, La.

Priv. Daniel W. Carroll, Canton; 28 years old; machinist; enlisted Sept. 17, 1862.

Priv. Edward S. Champney, Mansfield; 23 years old; machinist; enlisted Sept. 17, 1862.

Priv. Alonzo H. Clark, Sharon; 20 years old; bootmaker; enlisted Sept. 17, 1862. Died of disease June 15, 1863, at Brashear City, La.

Priv. John Coats, Stoughton; 38 years old; bootmaker; enlisted Sept. 17, 1862.

Priv. Albert Crossman, Stoughton; 25 years old; bootmaker; enlisted Sept. 17, 1862.

Priv. Jeremiah Crowley, Canton; 30 years old; blacksmith; enlisted Sept. 17, 1862. Wounded June 14, 1863, at Port Hudson, La.

Priv. Longbottom Crowther, Canton; 24 years old; spinner; enlisted Sept. 17, 1862. Died August 27, 1863. Regimental records do not indicate if death occurred in Louisiana or Massachusetts.

Priv. Rufus Daniels, Canton; 34 years old; baker; enlisted Sept. 17, 1862.

Priv. John Duffy, Easton; 25 years old; shovel maker; enlisted Sept. 17, 1862. Killed June 14, 1863, at Port Hudson, La. Also served in Company B, 4th Mass. Infantry for 3-month duty in 1861.

Priv. Stillman Dunakin, Sharon; 30 years old; knife maker; enlisted Sept. 17, 1862. Also served in Company A, 4th Mass. Infantry for 3-month duty in 1861.

Priv. Charles H. Eaton, Stoughton; 18 years old; clerk; enlisted Sept. 17, 1862. Taken prisoner June 14, 1863, at Port Hudson, La.

Priv. Owen Flood, Canton; 20 years old; bootmaker; enlisted Sept. 17, 1862.

Priv. William Foster, Canton; 19 years old; moulder; enlisted Sept. 17, 1862. Died of disease April 21, 1863, at New Orleans, La.

Priv. Hiram E. Gay, Stoughton; 18 years old; fisherman; enlisted Sept. 17, 1862.

Priv. John Geddis, Canton; 26 years old; laborer; enlisted Sept. 17, 1862. Died of disease April 12, 1863, at New Orleans, La.

Priv. Barney Glynn, Canton; 22 years old; blacksmith; enlisted Sept. 17, 1862.

Priv. Thomas Hearn, Canton; 35 years old; weaver; enlisted Sept. 17, 1862.

Priv. Charles H. Hersom, Canton; 31 years old; farmer; enlisted Sept. 17, 1862.

Priv. Alfred Hewins, Sharon; 22 years old; farmer; enlisted Sept. 17, 1862. Discharged due to disability March 16, 1863, at Boston, Mass. Also served in Company A, 4th Mass. Infantry for 3-month duty in 1861.

Priv. James Holliday, Canton; 43 years old; blacksmith; enlisted Sept. 17, 1862. Wounded June 14, 1863, at Port Hudson, La.

Priv. Frederick B. Howard, Canton; 23 years old; machinist; enlisted Sept. 17, 1862.

Priv. Alfred Hurd, Canton; 22 years old, machinist; enlisted Sept. 17, 1862.

Priv. Joseph Jenkins, Canton; 23 years old; machinist; enlisted Sept. 17, 1862. Died of disease Aug. 29, 1863.

Regimental records do not indicate if the death occurred in Louisiana or Massachusetts. Also served in Company A, 4th Mass. Infantry for 3-month duty in 1861.

Priv. George H. Johnson, Stoughton; 30 years old; painter; enlisted Sept. 17, 1862.

Priv. Ira Johnson, Sharon; 28 years old; farmer; enlisted Sept. 17, 1862. Taken prisoner June 23, 1863, at Brashear City, La.

Priv. John W. Kane, Sharon; 21 years old; bootmaker; enlisted Sept. 17, 1862.

Priv. Daniel Keefe, Canton; 25 years old; mechanic; enlisted Sept. 17, 1862.

Priv. Charles C. Knaggs, Canton; 18 years old; clerk; enlisted Sept. 17, 1862. Died Aug. 24, 1863. Regimental records do not indicate if the death occurred in Louisiana or Massachusetts.

Priv. Revilo R. Lamos, Canton; 21 years old; baker; enlisted Sept. 17, 1862.

Priv. Frederick E. Lane, Stoughton; 33 years old; bootmaker; enlisted Sept. 17, 1862.

Priv. John W. Lane, Stoughton; 21 years old; hostler; enlisted Sept. 17, 1862.

Priv. Nedebiah Lincoln, Canton; 31 years old; spinner; enlisted Sept. 17, 1862.

Priv. Frank Littlefield, Boston; 24 years old; farmer; enlisted Oct. 29, 1862. Taken prisoner June 23, 1863, at Brashear City, La.

Priv. Caleb B. Marsh, Stoughton; 30 years old; gilder; enlisted Sept. 17, 1862. Taken prisoner June 23, 1863, at Brashear City, La.

Priv. Martin McDonough, Stoughton; 23 years old, bootmaker; enlisted Sept. 17, 1862.

Priv. John McGinley, Canton; 18 years old; moulder; enlisted Sept. 17, 1862. Taken prisoner June 23, 1863, at Brashear City, La.

Priv. Anthony McGinty, Canton; 19 years old; bootmaker; enlisted Sept. 17, 1862. Discharged July 23, 1863, to reenlist in Company A, Headquarters Troops, XIX Army Corps, Dept. of the Gulf.

Priv. Thomas McLaughlin, Stoughton; 29 years old; bootmaker; enlisted Sept. 17, 1862. Died Aug. 1, 1863. Regimental records do not indicate where the death occurred, but it would have probably been in Louisiana.

Priv. Samuel W. Meserve, Canton; 34 years old; carpenter; enlisted Sept. 17, 1862.

Priv. John Mills, Stoughton; 27 years old; painter; enlisted Sept. 17, 1862.

Priv. William H. Morris, Canton; 28 years old; iron heater; enlisted Sept. 17, 1862. Taken prisoner June 23, 1863, Brashear City, La.

Priv. Stillman H. Morse, Sharon; 30 years old; mason; enlisted Sept. 17, 1862. Also served in Company A, 4th Mass. Infantry for 3-month duty in 1861.

Priv. Patrick Murphy, Canton; 21 years old; machinist; enlisted Sept. 17, 1862.

Priv. John Newman, Sharon; 19 years old; farmer; enlisted Sept. 17, 1862.

Priv. John O'Brien, Canton; 44 years old; stone mason; enlisted Sept. 17, 1862. Taken prisoner June 23, 1863, at Brashear City, La.

Priv. Timothy O'Flaherty, Canton; 24 years old; laborer; enlisted Sept. 17, 1862.

Priv. James Partington, Canton; 31 years old; dress tender; enlisted Sept. 17, 1862. Wounded June 14, 1863, at Port Hudson, La.

Priv. Ornan J. Perkins, Stoughton; 36 years old; bootmaker; enlisted Sept. 17, 1862. Wounded June 14, 1863, at Port Hudson, La.

Priv. Benjamin F. Phillips, Jr., Stoughton; 24 years old; farmer; enlisted Sept. 17, 1862.

Priv. Abram Poff, Sharon; 38 years old; teamster; enlisted Sept. 17, 1862. Taken prisoner June 23, 1863, at Brashear City, La.

Priv. Henry A. Presbrey, Canton; 20 years old; clerk; enlisted Sept. 17, 1862. Taken prisoner June 23, 1863, at Brashear City, La.

Priv. John F. Pye, Stoughton; 21 years old; blacksmith; enlisted Sept. 17, 1862.

Priv. Charles F. Richards, Sharon; 23 years old; bootmaker; enlisted Sept. 17, 1862. Taken prisoner June 23, 1863, at Brashear City, La.

Priv. Benjamin Rideout, Stoughton; 44 years old; farmer; enlisted Sept. 17, 1862. Taken prisoner June 23, 1863, at Brashear City, La. Died Aug. 2, 1863, at Port Hudson, La.

Priv. Michael E. Roach, Easton; 19 years old; shoemaker; enlisted Sept. 17, 1862. Wounded June 14, 1863, at Port Hudson, and died July 5, 1863, at New Orleans from wounds and disease.

Priv. David F. Sherman, Canton; 28 years old; machinist; enlisted Sept. 17, 1862.

Priv. Owen Shonsey, Canton; 23 years old; machinist; enlisted Sept. 17, 1862. Died of disease June 6, 1863, at Brashear City, La.

Priv. George W. Smith, Canton; 28 years old; moulder; enlisted Sept. 17, 1862.

Priv. Stephen H. Smith, Canton; 19 years old; weaver; enlisted Sept. 17, 1862. Killed June 14, 1863, at Port Hudson, La.

Priv. John D. Sullivan, Canton; 20 years old; farmer; enlisted Sept. 17, 1862. Taken prisoner June 23, 1863, at Brashear City, La.

Priv. Jabez Elmer Talbot, Stoughton; 18 years old; wheelwright; enlisted Sept. 17, 1862. Taken prisoner June 23, 1863, at Brashear City, La.

Priv. Samuel J. B. Taylor, Stoughton; 20 years old; bootmaker; enlisted Sept. 17, 1862. Died Aug. 15, 1863, probably in Louisiana.

Priv. Silas L. Thayer, Stoughton; 35 years old; farmer; enlisted Sept. 17, 1862. Wounded June 14, 1863, at Port Hudson, La.

Priv. Otis S. Tolman, Sharon; 25 years old; farmer; enlisted Sept. 17, 1862. Wounded June 14, 1863, at Port Hudson, La.

Priv. Edward B. Ware, Canton; 19 years old; clerk; enlisted Sept. 17, 1862.

Priv. George W. Warr, Canton; 18 years old; mechanic; enlisted Sept. 17, 1862. Deserted at Lakeville, Mass., Dec. 20, 1862.

Priv. Ellis Wentworth, Jr., Stoughton; 30 years old; bootmaker; enlisted Sept. 17, 1862. Taken prisoner June 23, 1863, at Brashear City, La.

Priv. Herbert O. Wentworth, Stoughton; 20 years old; enlisted Sept. 17, 1862. Taken prisoner June 23, 1863, at Brashear City, La.

Priv. Larra E. Wentworth, Canton; 18 years old; farmer; enlisted Sept. 17, 1862. Wounded June 14, 1863, at Port Hudson, La.

Priv. Asahel White, Canton; 45 years old; farmer; enlisted Sept. 17, 1862. Taken prisoner June 23, 1863, at Brashear City, La. Died July 26, 1863, in Louisiana.

Priv. Hiram H. White, Stoughton; 20 years old; bootmaker; enlisted Sept. 17, 1862. Died of disease June 30, 1863, at Baton Rouge, La.

Priv. Thomas G. White, Canton; 19 years old; carder; enlisted Sept. 17, 1862. Taken prisoner June 23, 1863, at Brashear City, La.

Priv. Lewis M. Williamson, Canton; 32 years old; farmer; enlisted Sept. 17, 1862. Taken prisoner June 23, 1863, at Brashear City, La.

COMPANY B

Captain George S. Merrill, Lawrence; 26 years old; editor; commissioned Captain, Dec. 8, 1862. Publisher and editor of the *Lawrence American* newspaper, postmaster, chairman of the National G.A.R. Pension Committee and Massachusetts State Insurance Commissioner. He died Feb. 17, 1900, survived by his wife, Sarah, and one daughter.

1st Lieut. John K. Tarbox, Lawrence; 24 years old; lawyer; commissioned 1st Lieut., Dec. 8, 1862. Editor of the *Lawrence Sentinel* newspaper, mayor of Lawrence, 1873–74 and member of the 44th U.S. Congress from the Seventh Massachusetts District.

2d Lieut. Albert F. Dow, Lawrence; 19 years old; clerk; commissioned 2d Lieut., Dec. 8, 1862. He was born Feb. 3, 1844, in Washington, N.H. He married in Jan. 1871 and had one son, Walter, born the same year. By 1914, Dow was the president of the Fall River Electric Light Company in Fall River, Mass., and was having great difficulty obtaining his Civil War pension. No birth record could be found, and he finally secured his payment by quoting two published genealogical and historical books concerning his family and birthplace.

1st Sergt. Perry M. Rice, Lawrence; 30 years old; turner; enlisted Aug. 26, 1862; promoted 1st Sergt., Dec. 8, 1862. Taken prisoner June 23, 1863, at Brashear City, La.

Sergt. Aaron A. Currier, Lawrence; 25 years old; carpenter; enlisted Aug. 26, 1862; promoted Sergt., Sept. 3, 1862. Currier built a number of buildings in Lawrence after he returned from Louisiana and was evidently very successful. He died Sept. 24, 1907, in North Andover, Mass., survived by his wife, Eliza, and six children: Addie, Carrie, Ella, John, Albert, and Herman. In 1916 a house fire took the life of his wife and daughter Ella.

Sergt. Joseph H. Morgan, Methuen; 24 years old; painter; enlisted Aug. 26, 1862; promoted Sergt., Sept. 3, 1862. Wounded May 22, 1863, on board the steamer *Louisiana Belle*.

Sergt. Hiram F. Lord, Springvale, Maine; 24 years old; carpenter; enlisted Aug. 26, 1862; promoted Sergt., Dec. 8, 1862. Lord married Mary Hurd in 1860 and fathered one child, Floral, born in 1861. He died Sept. 15, 1902, at Worcester, Mass.

Sergt. Gardner E. Wadlin, Lawrence; 30 years old; machinist; enlisted Aug. 26, 1862; promoted Sergt., Dec. 8, 1862. Wadlin was ill in Louisiana and in March 1863 was sent to the hospital in New Orleans. He did not peform any military duty and was unable to appear at the muster out of the 4th Massachusetts Infantry Regiment. On Sept. 14, 1863, he died in Lawrence, survived by his wife, Sarah, and one son, Frank.

Corpl. Rollin E. Harmon, Lawrence; 18 years old; student; enlisted Aug. 25, 1862; promoted Corpl., Sept. 1, 1862.

Corpl. William S. Greenough, Lawrence; 19 years old; student; enlisted Aug. 25, 1862; promoted Corpl., Sept. 1, 1862.

Corpl. John H. Gilman, Lawrence; 18 years old; carriage trimmer; enlisted Aug. 25, 1862; promoted Corpl., Sept. 1, 1862.

Corpl. Daniel F. Kiley, Lawrence; 18 years old; tailor; enlisted Aug. 26, 1862; promoted Corpl., Sept. 1, 1862. Wounded May 22, 1863, on the steamer *Louisiana Belle.*

Corpl. Philemon C. Parsons, Lawrence; 32 years old; operative; enlisted Aug. 27, 1862; promoted Corpl., Sept. 1, 1862. Taken prisoner June 23, 1863, at Brashear City, La.

Corpl. Thomas P. Wills, Lawrence; 20 years old; carpenter; enlisted Aug. 25, 1862; promoted Corpl., Dec. 8, 1862. Wounded May 22, 1863, on the steamer *Louisiana Belle.*

Corpl. Richard Crawshaw, Lawrence; 21 years old; piper; enlisted Aug. 27, 1862; promoted Corpl., Sept. 1, 1862. Killed June 14, 1863, at Port Hudson, La.

Corpl. Daniel G. Thyng, Lawrence; 22 years old; clerk; enlisted Aug. 26, 1862; promotion date to Corpl. is unknown. In March 1863, Thyng was in the General Hospital in Baton Rouge. He may have returned with the rest of his unit, or he may have been sent home earlier. He died Aug. 19, 1863, at Laconia, N.H.

Music, Clarence E. Drew, Lawrence; 16 years old; operative; enlisted Aug. 26, 1862. The roll books containing the names of the soldiers serving in the 4th Massachusetts Infantry Regiment are preserved in the Lawrence Public Library. After Private Drew's name is a notation that he was rejected as an incompetent musician. Since he was mustered out with the rest of his unit in 1863, I can only assume this notation reflects that he was not entitled to the extra stipend allotted to musicians. According to the roll book his middle name was Edgar, and it appears that was the name he used. At age 16 he was one of the youngest members of the unit. On May 10, 1864, he reenlisted in the 26th Mass. Infantry, Company I, and saw action in Virginia where he received a gunshot wound to his left ankle in Sept. of the same year. He was discharged May 25, 1865. On May 1, 1871, he married Angeline A. Sampson and in 1883 was having difficulty obtaining an invalid pension since the regimental doctors who had treated his wound were deceased as well as at least one of his regimental officers. The other officers could not be located. Drew died March 25, 1915.

Music, John F. Hayes, Lawrence; 18 years old; operative; enlisted Sept. 12, 1862. Taken prisoner June 23, 1863, at Brashear City, La. Hayes was aboard the steamer that left Louisiana on Aug. 4, 1863, but due to illness he was left at a hospital in Indianapolis, Ind., where he died Aug. 28, 1863.

Priv. James Adams, Lawrence; 20 years old; operative; enlisted Aug. 26, 1862. Died of disease in the General Hospital, New Orleans, La., on April 4, 1863.

Priv. James Aldred, Lawrence; 26 years old; operative; enlisted Aug. 27, 1862.

Priv. Currie Anderson, Lawrence; 24 years old; dresser; enlisted Aug. 26, 1862.

Priv. William Barnes, Lawrence; 32 years old; operative; enlisted Aug. 27, 1862.

Priv. John Baxter, Lawrence; 34 years old; operative; enlisted Aug. 26, 1862. Taken prisoner June 23, 1863, at Brashear City, La.

Priv. James Boardman, Lawrence; 42 years old; watchman; enlisted Aug. 26, 1862.

Priv. John Boyle, Lawrence; 22 years old; operative; enlisted Aug. 26, 1862.

Priv. Enoch Bradshaw, Lawrence; 32 years old; file grinder; enlisted Aug. 26, 1862. Wounded May 22, 1863, on the steamer *Louisiana Belle*.

Priv. John Brannon, Lawrence; 30 years old; spinner; enlisted Aug. 26, 1862. Taken prisoner June 23, 1863, at Brashear City, La.

Priv. James Buckley, Lawrence; 40 years old; operative; enlisted Sept. 8, 1862. Taken prisoner June 23, 1863, at Brashear City, La.

Priv. Henry Butler, Lawrence; 25 years old; engraver; enlisted Sept. 18, 1862.

Priv. Thomas M. Butler, Lawrence; 22 years old; operative; enlisted Aug. 27, 1862. Wounded May 22, 1863, on the steamer *Louisiana Belle*.

Priv. Daniel Carr, Jr., Lawrence; 38 years old; grocer; enlisted Aug. 26, 1862.

Priv. John Casey, Lawrence; 18 years old; operative; enlisted Aug. 27, 1862. Wounded June 14, 1863, Port Hudson, La.

Priv. Timothy Cleary, Lawrence; 18 years old; engraver; enlisted Aug. 26, 1862. Wounded May 22, 1863, on the steamer *Louisiana Belle*.

Priv. Thomas Coleman, Lawrence; 25 years old; spinner; enlisted Aug. 26, 1862.

Priv. Patrick Crosdale, Lawrence; 25 years old; wool sorter; enlisted Aug. 25, 1862. Deserted Oct. 20, 1862; was arrested and served his enlistment time in Company I, 30th Mass. Infantry.

Priv. John Cumnock, Lawrence; 26 years old; spinner; enlisted Aug. 26, 1862. Taken prisoner June 23, 1863, at Brashear City, La.

Priv. John Dennis, Lawrence; 32 years old; spinner; enlisted Aug. 26, 1862. Dennis is the probable author of the diary that prompted this book. The original company roll, at the Lawrence library, notes Dennis as a rank musician. That was not his designation at the time of enlistment, so his assignment as musician must have occurred sometime after his company was formed. I believe this designation was assigned to Dennis very early in 1863 after Private Drew was rejected as an incompetent musician. Dennis, who was born in Derby, England, had hazel eyes, brown hair and was 5 feet, 4 inches tall. In 1864 he reenlisted in the 2d Independent Battery, Mass. Light Artillery. He collected another bounty of $100 and was sent back to the Gulf area. On May 31, 1865, he was mustered out of service in Vicksburg, Miss. His health appears to have been very poor, and his last years were spent in and out of the National Soldiers Home in Togus, Maine. Dennis died March 22, 1911. He married twice. His first wife, Margaret, bore six children: John, Emma, Reanor, John A., Albert and Frank. Margaret died in 1875, and Sarah Buckley Edge became his second wife in 1876 when his youngest son would have been four years old. Sarah died in 1897.

Priv. David C. Dolloff, Lawrence; 36 years old; operative; enlisted Aug. 27, 1862.

Priv. Edward Dufresne, Lawrence; 26 years old; operative; enlisted Aug. 26, 1862.

Priv. William Duncan, Lawrence; 29 years old; operative; enlisted Aug. 27, 1862.

Priv. Joseph Dyer, Lawrence; 34 years old; spinner; enlisted Aug. 26, 1862.

Priv. J. Frank Eaton, Lawrence; 20 years old; clerk; enlisted Aug. 26, 1862.

Priv. James Edmondson, Lawrence; 29 years old; operative; enlisted Aug. 26, 1862. He died on the way home from Louisiana on Aug. 18, 1863, at Cleveland, Ohio.

Priv. James Ellis, Lawrence; 18 years old; operative; enlisted Aug. 26, 1862.

Priv. James Farquhar, Lawrence; 34 years old; operative; enlisted Aug. 26, 1862.

Priv. Charles Fish, Lawrence; 31 years old; operative; enlisted Aug. 26, 1862.

Priv. T. Allen French, Lawrence; 23 years old; clerk; enlisted Aug. 26, 1862.

Priv. Mark Froom, Lawrence; 24 years old; spinner; enlisted Aug. 27, 1862.

Priv. William Gearin, Lawrence; 20 years old; operative; enlisted Aug. 26, 1862.

Priv. John Grimshaw, Methuen; 36 years old; dyer; enlisted Aug. 26, 1862.

Priv. Federal B. Ham, Lawrence; 34 years old; mason; enlisted Aug. 26, 1862. Taken prisoner June 23, 1863, at Brashear City, La.

Priv. James Harper, Lawrence; 24 years old; operative; enlisted Aug. 26, 1862.

Priv. John G. Haskell, Lawrence; 31 years old; spinner; enlisted Aug. 27, 1862.

Priv. William Heap, Lawrence; 28 years old; operative; enlisted Aug. 26, 1862. Taken prisoner June 23, 1863, at Brashear City, La.

Priv. Nelson Hill, Lawrence; 18 years old; weaver; enlisted Oct. 2, 1862.

Priv. Arthur L. Homans, Plymouth, N.H.; 21 years old; carpenter; enlisted Aug. 26, 1862. Taken prisoner June 23, 1863, at Brashear City, La.

Priv. Thomas Horrocks, Lawrence; 34 years old; weaver; enlisted Sept. 3, 1862. Wounded June 14, 1863, at Port Hudson, La.

Priv. George Horton, Lawrence; 34 years old; operative; enlisted Aug. 30, 1862. Died of disease May 9, 1863, at the General Hospital, New Orleans, La.

Priv. Joseph Jackson, Lawrence; 34 years old; operative; enlisted Aug. 26, 1862. Taken prisoner June 23, 1863, at Brashear City, La.

Priv. Samuel Jackson, Lawrence; 29 years old; operative; enlisted Aug. 26, 1862.

Priv. Samuel Johnson, Lawrence; 26 years old; trimmer; enlisted Aug. 27, 1862.

Priv. Stephen P. Kimball, Lawrence; 31 years old; painter; enlisted Aug. 25, 1862. Taken prisoner June 23, 1863, at Brashear City, La.

Priv. Benjamin Lakey, Lawrence; 23 years old; roll coverer; enlisted Aug. 26, 1862.

Priv. Joseph Lawlor, Lawrence; 18 years old; operative; enlisted Aug. 26, 1862. Taken prisoner June 23, 1863, at Brashear City, La.

Priv. Charles A. Lyons, Lawrence; 37 years old; carpenter; enlisted Aug. 27, 1862. Taken prisoner June 23, 1863, at Brashear City, La.

Priv. Michael Maragan, Lawrence; 19 years old; laborer; enlisted Aug. 26, 1862.

Priv. Frederick Marquardt, Methuen; 29 years old; no occupation listed; enlisted Dec. 10, 1862.

Priv. Michael McCulloch, Lawrence; 20 years old; operative; enlisted Aug. 27, 1862.

Priv. Edward McGuire, Lawrence; 37 years old; operative; enlisted Aug. 26, 1862. Taken prisoner June 23, 1863, at Brashear City, La.

Priv. Conrad Miller, Lawrence; 23 years old; weaver; enlisted Sept. 9, 1862.

Priv. James H. Mills, Methuen; 35 years old; engraver; enlisted Aug. 26, 1862. Died of disease June 16, 1863, at Brashear City, La.

Priv. Henry Morgan, Methuen; 21 years old; painter; enlisted Aug. 26, 1862.

Priv. William Morgan, Methuen; 23 years old; painter; enlisted Aug. 26, 1862. Morgan made it home from Louisiana but died Aug. 24, 1863, just a few days before his unit was to be mustered out.

Priv. George W. Morse, Lawrence; 21 years old; clerk; enlisted Aug. 25, 1862. Morse was transferred to the 48th Mass. Infantry, Dec. 11, 1862.

Priv. John Oliver, Lawrence; 34 years old; spinner; enlisted Aug. 26, 1862. Taken prisoner June 23, 1863, at Brashear City, La.

Priv. Noah Parkman, Lawrence; 29 years old; no occupation given; enlisted Aug. 26, 1862. Parkman was discharged Sept. 24, 1862, for disability.

Priv. Thomas A. Parsons, Lawrence; 39 years old; lawyer; enlisted Aug. 25, 1862.

Priv. A. Franklin Perkins, Bridgewater; 29 years old; carpenter; enlisted Aug. 27, 1862.

Priv. Robert Pickles, Lawrence; 36 years old; operative; enlisted Aug. 26, 1862.

Priv. J. Frank Place, Lawrence; 25 years old; editor; enlisted Aug. 25, 1862.

Priv. Edgar G. Pratt, Lawrence; 19 years old; mason; enlisted Aug. 26, 1862. Wounded June 14, 1863, at Port Hudson, La.

Priv. Orlando Rawson, Lawrence; 32 years old; operative; enlisted Aug. 26, 1862. Taken prisoner June 23, 1863, at Brashear City, La. He died on his way home Aug. 16, 1863, at Indianapolis, Ind.

Priv. Walter S. Riddell, Lawrence; 31 years old; operative; enlisted Aug. 26, 1862. Riddell drowned Dec. 27, 1862, while aboard the ship moving his unit to New York City.

Priv. John Rowe, Lawrence; 30 years old; dresser; enlisted Aug. 26, 1862.

Priv. W. Frank Russ, Lawrence; 23 years old; shoemaker; enlisted Aug. 26, 1862.

Priv. Philip Ryan, Lawrence; 37 years old; occupation not given; enlisted Aug. 25, 1862. Deserted Nov. 1, 1862.

Priv. Warren Sargent, Lawrence; 27 years old; carpenter; enlisted Aug. 26, 1862. Wounded May 22, 1863, on the steamer *Louisiana Belle*.

Priv. Charles Shaw, Lawrence; 18 years old; machinist; enlisted Aug. 27, 1862. Wounded May 22, 1863, on the steamer *Louisiana Belle*.

Priv. John Shaw, Lawrence; 37 years old; operative; enlisted Aug. 26, 1862. Taken prisoner June 23, 1863, at Brashear City, La.

Priv. Augustus Sheppard, Quebec, Canada; 20 years old; wheelwright; enlisted Dec. 10, 1862. Died Aug. 3, 1863, at Port Hudson, La.

Priv. Stephen A. Simmons, Lawrence; 25 years old; machinist; enlisted Aug. 27, 1862.

Priv. Hiram A. Stearns, Lawrence; 28 years old; wool comber; enlisted Aug. 26, 1862. Also served in Company I, 6th Mass. Infantry for 3-month duty in 1861.

Priv. Isaac Stevens, Jr., Lawrence; 19 years old; music teacher; enlisted Aug. 25, 1862. Stevens, one of eight children, returned to Massachusetts in Aug. 1863 and married Millie Cook. They were divorced in April 1875, and she retained custody of their son, Joseph Roy Stevens. In 1889 he married Anna Baumann in Milwaukee, Wisc., and died June 12, 1929. He is buried in Oakwood Cemetery, Chicago, Ill.

Priv. Michael F. Sullivan, Lawrence; 21 years old; harness maker; enlisted Aug. 26, 1862. Wounded June 14, 1863, at Port Hudson, La.

Priv. Edward Terreau, Lawrence; 28 years old; operative; enlisted Oct. 2, 1862.

Priv. Isaac S. Varnam, Lawrence; 44 years old; paper maker; enlisted Sept. 15, 1862. On March 5, 1863, Varnam died at a hospital in Carrollton, La.

Priv. Ralph Varnam, Lawrence; 25 years old; carpenter; enlisted Aug. 26, 1862. Taken prisoner June 23, 1863, at Brashear City, La.

Priv. Joseph Walsh, Lawrence; 23 years old; box maker; enlisted Sept. 6, 1862.

Priv. Charles O. Webster, Lawrence; 19 years old; clerk; enlisted Aug. 25, 1862.

Priv. Robert Whatmore, Lawrence; 38 years old; spinner; enlisted Aug. 26, 1862. Taken prisoner June 23, 1863, at Brashear City, La.

Priv. William Whitmore, Lawrence; 28 years old; operative; enlisted Aug. 26, 1862. Wounded June 14, 1863, at Port Hudson, La.

Priv. James Winning, Lawrence; 32 years old; operative; enlisted Aug. 26, 1862.

COMPANY C

Captain Seneca R. Thomas, Middleboro; 39 years old; farmer; commissioned Sept. 3, 1862.

1st Lieut. Daniel F. Wood, Middleboro; 35 years old; painter; commissioned Sept. 3, 1862. Also served in Company G, 4th Mass. Infantry for 3-month duty in 1861.

2d Lieut. James M. Sampson, Lakeville; 28 years old; clerk; commissioned Sept. 3, 1862. Taken prisoner June 23, 1863, at Brashear City, La.

1st Sergt. Sargent S. Swett, Middleboro; 40 years old; painter; enlisted Sept. 19, 1862; appointed 1st Sergt., Dec. 6, 1862. Taken prisoner June 23, 1863, at Brashear City, La.

Sergt. Frederic E. Wood, Middleboro; 27 years old; painter; enlisted Sept. 19, 1862; appointed Sergt., Dec. 6, 1862.

Sergt. Orlando H. Shaw, Middleboro; 35 years old; farmer; enlisted Sept. 19, 1862; appointed Sergt., Dec. 6, 1862.

Sergt. J. Horace Soule, Middleboro; 24 years old; teacher; enlisted Sept. 19, 1862; appointed Sergt., Dec. 6, 1862.

Sergt. Dura T. Weston, Middleboro; 22 years old; carpenter; enlisted Sept. 19, 1862; appointed Sergt., Dec. 6, 1862. Taken prisoner June 23, 1863, at Brashear City, La.

Corpl. Edward Hackett, Lakeville; 38 years old; carpenter; enlisted Sept. 19, 1862; appointed Corpl., Dec. 6, 1862.

Corpl. Erastus E. Gay, Middleboro; 34 years old; miller; enlisted Sept. 19, 1862; appointed Corpl., Dec. 6, 1862. Taken prisoner June 23, 1863, at Brashear City, La.

Corpl. Sylvanus Mendall, Middleboro; 31 years old; sawyer; enlisted Sept. 19, 1862; appointed Corpl., Dec. 6, 1862.

Corpl. Dennis Shaw, Middleboro; 51 years old; moulder; enlisted Sept. 19, 1862; appointed Corpl., Dec. 6, 1862. Taken prisoner June 23, 1863, at Brashear City, La.

Corpl. Isaac E. Macomber, Middleboro; 35 years old; shoemaker; enlisted Sept. 19, 1862; appointed Corpl., Dec. 6, 1862. Wounded June 14, 1863, at Port Hudson, La.

Corpl. David A. Tucker, Middleboro; 25 years old; spool maker; enlisted Sept. 19, 1862; appointed Corpl., Dec. 6, 1862.

Corpl. George W. Barrows, Middleboro; 27 years old; painter; enlisted Sept. 19, 1862; appointed Corpl., Dec. 6, 1862. Taken prisoner June 23, 1863, at Brashear City, La.

Corpl. Sylvester R. Swett, Plymouth; 32 years old; painter; enlisted Sept. 19, 1862; appointed Corpl., Dec. 6, 1862. Taken prisoner June 23, 1863, at Brashear City, La.

Corpl. Francis S. Thomas, Middleboro; 23 years old; hostler; enlisted Sept. 19, 1862. Died Mar. 8, 1863, in the hospital in Carrollton, La.

Music William W. Atwood, Middleboro; 18 years old; artist; enlisted Sept. 19, 1862. Taken prisoner June 23, 1863, at Brashear City, La.

Music Joshua M. Jenney, Middleboro; 18 years old; farmer; enlisted Sept. 19, 1862. Taken prisoner June 23, 1863, at Brashear City, La.

Music Alexander Brand, Dartmouth; 20 years old; farmer; enlisted Dec. 5, 1862. Deserted Dec. 26, 1862, from Camp Hooker, Lakeville, Mass.

Priv. Asa R. Adams, Middleboro; 28 years old; moulder; enlisted Sept. 19, 1862.

Priv. Andrew Alden, Middleboro; 24 years old; shoemaker; enlisted Sept. 19, 1862. Taken prisoner June 23, 1863, at Brashear City, La.

Priv. Isaac Alger, Middleboro; 43 years old; bootmaker; enlisted Sept. 19, 1862. Taken prisoner June 23, 1863, at Brashear City, La.

Priv. Myron E. Alger, Middleboro; 19 years old; bootmaker; enlisted Sept. 19, 1862. Taken prisoner June 23, 1863, at Brashear City, La. Died July 10, 1863, at Brashear City, La.

Priv. John C. Ashley, Lakeville; 25 years old; shoemaker; enlisted Sept. 19, 1862.

Priv. William C. Ashley, Easton; 34 years old; farmer; enlisted Sept. 19, 1862.

Priv. William Barney, Lakeville; 22 years old; farmer; enlisted Sept. 19, 1862. Taken prisoner June 23, 1863, at Brashear City, La.

Priv. Earle Bennett, Middleboro; 27 years old; box maker; enlisted Sept. 19, 1862. Taken prisoner June 23, 1863, at Brashear City, La.

Priv. Grover Bennett, Middleboro; 18 years old; farmer; enlisted Sept. 19, 1862. Taken prisoner June 23, 1863, at Brashear City, La.

Priv. Elisha Benson, Middleboro; 44 years old; landlord; enlisted Sept. 19, 1862.

Priv. Sylvanus Bisbee, Middleboro; 30 years old; shoemaker; enlisted Sept. 19, 1862.

Priv. Augustus N. J. Buchel, Middleboro; 28 years old; mechanic; enlisted Sept. 19, 1862.

Priv. David H. Burgess, Middleboro; 17 years old; shoemaker; enlisted Sept. 19, 1862. The only records available indicate he died about Aug. 28, 1863, in Massachusetts. Evidently, he returned from Louisiana but lived a very short time after his arrival.

Priv. William B. Burt, Middleboro; 29 years old; shoemaker; enlisted Sept. 19, 1862.

Priv. Edwin M. Cole, Middleboro; 32 years old; mechanic; enlisted Sept. 19, 1862. Taken prisoner June 23, 1863, at Brashear City, La.

Priv. William H. Cole, Lakeville; 34 years old; shoemaker; enlisted Sept. 19, 1862. Taken prisoner June 23, 1863, at Brashear City, La. Died of disease Aug. 9, 1863, at New Orleans, La.

Priv. William A. Coombs, Middleboro; 26 years old; shoemaker; enlisted Sept. 19, 1862. Taken prisoner June 23, 1863, at Brashear City, La.

Priv. Richard Cox, Middleboro; 29 years old; painter; enlisted Sept. 19, 1862. Taken prisoner June 23, 1863, at Brashear City, La.

Priv. John Doyle, Dartmouth; 23 years old; occupation not given; enlisted Dec. 11, 1862. Deserted Dec. 12, 1862, from Camp Hooker, Lakeville, Mass.

Priv. William Eaton, Jr., Middleboro; 28 years old; shoemaker; enlisted Sept. 19, 1862. Died June 21, 1863, in New Orleans, La., from wounds received at Port Hudson on June 14, 1863.

Priv. John D. P. Emery, Lakeville; 34 years old; shoemaker; enlisted Sept. 19, 1862.

Priv. Michael Farrell, Dartmouth; 23 years old; occupation not given; enlisted Dec. 13, 1862. Deserted Dec. 16, 1862, from Camp Hooker, Lakeville, Mass.

Priv. Thomas W. Finney, Middleboro; 24 years old; bootmaker; enlisted Sept. 19, 1862.

Priv. Asa M. Franklin, Middleboro; 23 years old; jeweler; enlisted Sept. 19, 1862.

Priv. Joseph Grant, Dartmouth; 23 years old; occupation not given; enlisted Dec. 9, 1862. Deserted Dec. 11, 1862, from Camp Hooker, Lakeville, Mass.

Priv. Jonathan L. Hall, Middleboro; 22 years old; shoemaker; enlisted Sept. 19, 1862. Taken prisoner June 23, 1863, at Brashear City, La.

Priv. Daniel Handy, Middleboro; 43 years old; farmer; enlisted Sept. 19, 1862. Taken prisoner June 23, 1863, at Brashear City, La.

Priv. Reuben Harlow, Middleboro; 44 years old; teamster; enlisted Sept. 19, 1862. Taken prisoner June 23, 1863, at Brashear City, La. Harlow served in Company B, 4th Mass. Infantry for a 3-month term at the start of the war and in Company G, 20th Mass. Infantry, after his time expired in Company C, 4th Mass. Infantry.

Priv. Reuben A. Harlow, Middleboro; 18 years old; farmer; enlisted Sept. 19, 1862. Taken prisoner June 23, 1863, at Brashear City, La.

Priv. Thompson R. Haskins, Lakeville; 46 years old; shoemaker; enlisted Sept. 19, 1862.

Priv. Levi Hathaway, Middleboro; 37 years old; carpenter; enlisted Sept. 19, 1862. Hathaway started home from Louisiana but died Aug. 19, 1863, of disease at Indianapolis, Ind.

Priv. Conrad J. Herman, Middleboro; 18 years old; farmer; enlisted Sept. 19, 1862.

Priv. George H. Herman, Middleboro; 26 years old; farmer; enlisted Sept. 19, 1862. Taken prisoner June 23, 1863, Brasher City, La.

Priv. Benjamin F. Holloway, Lakeville; 42 years old; farmer; enlisted Sept. 19, 1862. Holloway was wounded at Port Hudson on June 14, 1863, and died on June 15, 1863.

Priv. Charles H. Holmes, Middleboro; 24 years old; painter; enlisted Sept. 19, 1862.

Priv. Nahum W. Keith, Middleboro; 27 years old; shoemaker; enlisted Sept. 19, 1862.

Priv. Lysander W. Mitchell, Bridgewater; 18 years old; farmer; enlisted Sept. 19, 1862. Died of disease on July 31, 1863, at Port Hudson, La.

Priv. William Mitchell, Middleboro; 29 years old; carpenter; enlisted Sept. 19, 1862.

Priv. Michael Morrison, Dartmouth; 21 years old; occupation not given; enlisted Dec. 9, 1862. Deserted Dec. 27, 1862, from Camp Hooker, Lakeville, Mass.

Priv. Andrew Osborne, Lakeville; 18 years old; nailer; enlisted Sept. 19, 1862. Taken prisoner June 23, 1863, at Brashear City, La.

Priv. Charles E. Pierce, Lakeville; 18 years old; farmer; enlisted Oct. 21, 1862.

Priv. Charles T. Pierce, Lakeville; 44 years old; carpenter; enlisted Oct. 20, 1862.

Priv. Charles F. Plummer, Boston; 23 years old; occupation not given; enlisted Dec. 5, 1862. Deserted Dec. 12, 1862, from Camp Hooker, Lakeville, Mass.

Priv. Harvey C. Pratt, Middleboro; 32 years old; shoemaker; enlisted Sept. 19, 1862.

Priv. Cornelius Redding, Middleboro; 31 years old; miner; enlisted Sept. 19, 1862.

Priv. Morton Robbins, Middleboro; 37 years old; shoemaker; enlisted Sept. 19, 1862. Taken prisoner June 23, 1863, at Brashear City, La.

Priv. Andrew P. Rogers, Middleboro; 22 years old; mariner; enlisted Sept. 19, 1862.

Priv. William H. Rogers, Middleboro; 28 years old; shoemaker; enlisted Sept. 19, 1862. Taken prisoner June 23, 1863, at Brashear City, La.

Priv. Horatio N. Sampson, Lakeville; 24 years old; farmer; enlisted Sept. 19, 1862. Taken prisoner June 23, 1863, at Brashear City, La.

Priv. E. Howard Shaw, Middleboro; 31 years old; shoemaker; enlisted Sept. 19, 1862. Taken prisoner June 23, 1863, at Brashear City, La.

Priv. Henry L. Shaw, Middleboro; 31 years old; farmer; enlisted Sept. 19, 1862. Wounded June 14, 1863, at Port Hudson, La., and died of his wounds Oct. 6, 1863, at Middleboro, Mass.

Priv. Joseph B. Shaw, Middleboro; 32 years old; blacksmith; enlisted Sept. 19, 1862.

Priv. William Sheridan, Dartmouth; 22 years old; occupation not given; enlisted Dec. 11, 1862. Deserted Dec. 12, 1862, from Camp Hooker, Lakeville, Mass.

Priv. Winslow B. Sherman, Plymouth; 42 years old; laborer; enlisted Oct. 29, 1862. Taken prisoner June 23, 1863, at Brashear City, La.

Priv. Ephraim Simmons, Middleboro; 40 years old; farmer; enlisted Sept. 19, 1862. Died May 25, 1863, at Brashear City, La., of disease.

Priv. Stillman S. Smith, Middleboro; 20 years old; butcher; enlisted Sept. 19, 1862. Discharged on Feb. 26, 1863, for disability, at Boston, Mass.

Priv. Rodney E. Southworth, Middleboro; 22 years old; painter; enlisted Sept. 19, 1862.

Priv. Alfred O. Standish, Middleboro; 37 years old; moulder; enlisted Sept. 19, 1862. Taken prisoner June 23, 1863, at Brashear City, La.

Priv. John Sullivan, Middleboro; 22 years old; student; enlisted Sept. 19, 1862.

Priv. John Sullivan, II, Dartmouth; 21 years old; occupation not given; enlisted Dec. 11, 1862. Deserted Dec. 12, 1862, from Camp Hooker, Lakeville, Mass.

Priv. Henry A. Swift, Middleboro; 44 years old; enlisted Sept. 19, 1862. Taken prisoner June 23, 1863, at Brashear City, La.

Priv. Andrew E. Thomas, Middleboro; 22 years old; farmer; enlisted Sept. 19, 1862. Taken prisoner June 23, 1863, Brashear City, La. Died June 27, 1863, Brashear City, La.

Priv. Joseph Thomas, Middleboro; 19 years old; farmer; enlisted Sept. 19, 1862. Died Aug. 1, 1863, Port Hudson, La.

Priv. Stephen F. Thomas, Middleboro; 19 years old; moulder; enlisted Sept. 19, 1862. Died May 1, 1863, of disease in a hospital in New Orleans, La.

Priv. Winslow Thomas, Middleboro; 45 years old; moulder; enlisted Sept. 19, 1862. Taken prisoner June 23, 1863, Brashear City, La.

Priv. Alva C. Tinkham, Middleboro; 18 years old; mariner; enlisted Sept. 19, 1862. Taken prisoner June 23, 1863, at Brashear City, La. Died July 15, 1863, at Brashear City, La.

Priv. James H. Waterman, Middleboro; 38 years old; laborer; enlisted Sept. 19, 1862.

Priv. Thomas E. Waterman, Middleboro; 33 years old; shoemaker; enlisted Sept. 19, 1862. Taken prisoner June 23, 1863, Brashear City, La.

Priv. Dura Weston Jr., Middleboro; 45 years old; carpenter; enlisted Sept. 19, 1862.

Priv. Charles M. Wilbur, Middleboro; 31 years old; mechanic; enlisted Sept. 19, 1862.

Priv. Narcissus Williams, Lakeville; 28 years old; shoemaker; enlisted Sept. 19, 1862. Died of disease June 11, 1863, at Brashear City, La.

Priv. Samuel Williams, Lakeville; 23 years old; farmer; enlisted Sept. 19, 1862. Taken prisoner June 23, 1863, Brashear City, La.

Priv. Edward W. Wood, Middleboro; 22 years old; student; enlisted Sept. 19, 1862.

Priv. Jacob Wood, Middleboro; 40 years old; mariner; enlisted Sept. 19, 1862. Wounded June 14, 1863, at Port Hudson, La.

Priv. Joseph Young, Stoughton; 43 years old; farmer; enlisted Sept. 19, 1862.

COMPANY D

Captain Hiram C. Alden, Randolph; 36 years old; boot cutter; commissioned Sept. 1, 1862.

1st Lieut. Myron W. Hollis, Randolph; 25 years old; bootmaker; commissioned Sept. 1, 1862. Also served in Company D, 4th Mass Infantry for 3-month duty in 1861.

2d Lieut. Edmund Cottle, Randolph; 24 years old; teacher; commissioned Sept. 1, 1862. Wounded June 14, 1863, at Port Hudson, La. Also served in Company D, 4th Mass. Infantry for 3-month duty in 1861.

1st Sergt. George E. Knight, Randolph; 24 years old; boot cutter; enlisted Sept. 17, 1862. Also served in Company D, 4th Mass. Infantry for 3-month duty in 1861. Taken prisoner June 23, 1863, at Brashear City, La.

Sergt. William H. Alden, Randolph; 23 years old; boot cutter; enlisted Sept. 17, 1862. Also served in Company D, 4th Mass. Infantry for 3-month duty in 1861.

Sergt. Clark Wentworth, East Stoughton; 28 years old; painter; enlisted Sept. 17, 1862; promoted Sergt., April 17, 1863. Taken prisoner June 23, 1863, at Brashear City, La.

Sergt. Charles W. Tower, Randolph; 20 years old; student; enlisted Sept. 17, 1862; promoted Sergt., March 3, 1863.

Sergt. Joseph W. Thayer, Randolph; 28 years old; bootmaker; enlisted Sept. 17, 1862; promoted Sergt., July 19, 1863.

Sergt. Leonard Pierce, Randolph; 33 years old; bootmaker; enlisted Sept. 17, 1862; did not ship out to Louisiana but was discharged March 3, 1863, at Boston due to disability.

Sergt. Matthew Clark, Jr., Randolph; 21 years old; student; enlisted Sept. 17, 1862. Died April 17, 1863, of disease in Berwick City, La.

Sergt. William F. Gill, Randolph; 23 years old; clerk; enlisted Sept. 17, 1862. Died of disease July 19, 1863, at Arsenal Hospital in Baton Rouge, La.

Corpl. John Palmer, East Stoughton; 25 years old; carpenter, enlisted Sept. 17, 1862. Member of the color guard.

Corpl. James F. Dargan, Randolph; 19 years old; boot treer; enlisted Sept. 17, 1862. Wounded June 14, 1863, at Port Hudson, La. Dargan wrote a diary covering his experiences in the Civil War that eventually surfaced in an edited version in California. He enlisted at 19 with the consent of his parents and was granted an invalid pension for the head gunshot wound he received at Port Hudson. He and his widow also tried for years to obtain additional pension money for a condition he claimed was the result of an injury in Louisiana. Although it is difficult to determine the exact medical problem from his pension applications, it appears he suffered from a severe scrotal rupture or perhaps testicular cancer. He married Bridget Grace, Sept. 20, 1868, and fathered four children: Catharine, Margaret Ann, James, and William Patrick. Dargan died at the age of 39 on Sept. 19, 1882, in Buffalo, N.Y. His death certificate states the cause of death as uremic poisoning.

Corpl. Lyman Upham, Randolph; 22 years old; boot cutter; enlisted Sept. 17, 1862. Taken prisoner June 23, 1863, at Brashear City, La. Also served in Company D, 4th Mass. Infantry for 3-month duty in 1861.

Corpl. Richmond T. Pratt, Randolph; 27 years old; bootmaker; enlisted Sept. 17, 1862; promoted Corpl., March 3, 1863.

Corpl. Charles H. Belcher, Randolph; 22 years old; carpenter; enlisted Sept. 17, 1862; promoted Corpl., March 30, 1863. Wounded June 14, 1863, at Port Hudson, La.

Corpl. Orrin A. Reynolds, Randolph; 24 years old; boot manufacturer; enlisted Sept. 17, 1862; promoted Corpl., April 17, 1863. Taken prisoner June 23, 1863, at Brashear City, La.

Corpl. George C. Spear, Randolph; 20 years old; string maker; enlisted Sept. 17, 1862; promoted Corpl., April 19, 1863.

Corpl. Angelo A. Burbank, Randolph; 20 years old; boot stitcher; enlisted Sept. 17, 1862; promoted Corpl., April 19, 1863.

Corpl. William H. Shedd, Randolph; 22 years old; bootmaker; enlisted Sept. 17, 1862. Died of disease on March 30, 1863, in the General Hospital, Baton Rouge, La.

Corpl. George Smith, Randolph; 45 years old; bootmaker; enlisted Sept. 17, 1862. Died of disease June 17, 1863, in the Regimental Hospital, Brashear City, La.

Music Charles H. Thayer, Randolph; 18 years old; bootmaker; enlisted Sept. 17, 1862. Taken prisoner June 23, 1863, at Brashear City, La. Thayer was a drummer.

Wagoner Ezra R. Payne, Randolph; 36 years old; laborer; enlisted Sept. 17, 1862. Payne was an ambulance driver for the regiment.

Priv. Lucas W. Alden, Randolph; 26 years old; butcher; enlisted Sept. 17, 1862. Alden also played in the band and served in the ambulance corps during the battle of Port Hudson.

Priv. Horatio B. Arnold, Randolph; 19 years old; farmer; enlisted Sept. 17, 1862.

Priv. James Barry, Randolph; 22 years old; boot treer; enlisted Sept. 17, 1862. Taken prisoner June 23, 1863, at Brashear City, La.

Priv. Seth C. Bean, Randolph; 36 years old; bootmaker; enlisted Sept. 17, 1862. Taken prisoner June 23, 1863, at Brashear City, La. Died at Randolph, Mass., on Aug. 23, 1863.

Priv. Francis A. Belcher, Randolph; 20 years old; clerk; enlisted Sept. 17, 1862.

Priv. Richmond Blencowe, Randolph; 21 years old; boot cutter; enlisted Sept. 17, 1862. Died of disease June 25, 1863, at the Regimental Hospital in Brashear City, La.

Priv. William W. Blencowe, Randolph; 23 years old; boot cutter; enlisted Sept. 17, 1862. Taken prisoner June 23, 1863, at Brashear City, La. Also served Company D, 4th Mass. Infantry for 3-month duty in 1861.

Priv. Daniel Brosnihan, Randolph; 25 years old; bootmaker; enlisted Sept. 17, 1862.

Priv. Joseph W. Bryant, East Stoughton; 22 years old; bootmaker; enlisted Sept. 17, 1862.

Priv. Frederick Chandler, Randolph; 23 years old; boot fitter; enlisted Sept. 17, 1862.

Priv. Isaac Clark, Randolph; 43 years old; farmer; enlisted Sept. 17, 1862.

Priv. Orlando T. Crane, East Stoughton; 31 years old; blacksmith; enlisted Sept. 17, 1862.

Priv. George H. Croak, Randolph; 19 years old; boot cutter; enlisted Sept. 17, 1862. Died of disease June 1, 1863, at the Regimental Hospital, Brashear City, La.

Priv. Daniel D. Dennehy, Randolph; 21 years old; boot fitter; enlisted Sept. 17, 1862.

Priv. George B. Deuch, Randolph; 29 years old; painter; enlisted Sept. 17, 1862. Deuch was detailed as a mail carrier for the regiment in Louisiana.

Priv. James C. Driscoll, Randolph; 19 years old; waiter; enlisted Sept. 17, 1862. Taken prisoner June 23, 1863, at Brashear City, La.

Priv. James Early, Randolph; 29 years old; bootmaker; enlisted Sept. 17, 1862. Taken prisoner June 23, 1863, at Brashear City, La.

Priv. George Eddy, Randolph; 23 years old; bootmaker; enlisted Sept. 17, 1862.

Priv. John Foley, Randolph; 26 years old; bootmaker; enlisted Sept. 17, 1862.

Priv. James D. Fox, Randolph; 19 years old; bootmaker; enlisted Sept. 17, 1862. Taken prisoner June 23, 1863, at Brashear City, La.

Priv. Patrick Green, Randolph; 18 years old; bootmaker; enlisted Sept. 17, 1862. Died in Randolph sometime prior to 1880.

Priv. Peter B. Hand, Randolph; 19 years old; bootmaker; enlisted Sept. 17, 1862. Taken prisoner June 23, 1863, at Brashear City, La.

Priv. Thomas F. Hand, Randolph; 24 years old; bootmaker; enlisted Sept. 17, 1862. Hand was detailed as a cook.

Priv. James F. Harris, Randolph; 28 years old; bootmaker; enlisted Sept. 17, 1862. Taken prisoner June 23, 1863, at Brashear City, La.

Priv. John Harris, Randolph; 22 years old; bootmaker; enlisted Sept. 17, 1862.

Priv. Jeremiah Healy, Randolph; 30 years old; bootmaker; enlisted Sept. 17, 1862. Deserted Sept. 30, 1862, from Camp Hooker in Lakeville, Mass.

Priv. Samuel R. Hodge, Randolph; 26 years old; bootmaker; enlisted Sept. 17, 1862. Taken prisoner June 23, 1863, at Brashear City, La.

Priv. Hiram Holbrook, Randolph; 19 years old; bootmaker; enlisted Sept. 17, 1862. Taken prisoner June 23, 1863, at Brashear City, La.

Priv. Seth Holbrook, Randolph; 23 years old; bootmaker; enlisted Sept. 17, 1862.

Priv. Edgar Howard, Randolph; 18 years old; student; enlisted Sept. 17, 1862.

Priv. Henry B. Howard, Randolph; 25 years old; carpenter; enlisted Sept. 17, 1862.

Priv. Henry M. Howard, Randolph; 31 years old; bootmaker; enlisted Sept. 17, 1862.

Priv. Simeon Howard, Randolph; 41 years old; bootmaker, enlisted Sept. 17, 1862.

Priv. James Jordan, Randolph; 28 years old; boot treer; enlisted Sept. 17, 1862.

Priv. John Kelliher, Randolph; 23 years old; bootmaker; enlisted Sept. 17, 1862.

Priv. Edward Kiernan, Randolph; 24 years old; bootmaker; enlisted Sept. 17, 1862. Deserted Nov. 1, 1862, from Camp Hooker, Lakeville, Mass. Kiernan also served in the 1st New Jersey Heavy Artillery under the name of Edward Arley.

Priv. Moses D. Linfield, East Stoughton; 22 years old; bootmaker; enlisted Sept. 17, 1862.

Priv. Charles C. Littlefield, East Stoughton; 31 years old; bootmaker; enlisted Sept. 17, 1862.

Priv. George F. Littlefield, East Stoughton; 18 years old; student; enlisted Sept. 17, 1862.

Priv. Isaac J. Lovering, Randolph; 25 years old; teamster; enlisted Sept. 17, 1862. Wounded June 14, 1863, at Port Hudson, La. Also served in Company D, 4th Mass. Infantry for 3-month duty in 1861.

Priv. John Mahony, Randolph; 31 years old; bootmaker; enlisted Sept. 17, 1862.

Priv. Albert M. May, Randolph; 19 years old; bootmaker; enlisted Sept. 17, 1862. Died of disease July 20, 1863, in the General Hospital, Baton Rouge, La.

Priv. Thomas McGrath, Randolph; 25 years old; bootmaker; enlisted Sept. 17, 1862.

Priv. Edward McLaughlan, Randolph; 45 years old; bootmaker; enlisted Sept. 17, 1862.

Priv. Peter McMahon, Randolph; 24 years old; bootmaker; enlisted Sept. 17, 1862.

Priv. Edward Morgan, Randolph; 36 years old; bootmaker; enlisted Sept. 17, 1862. Wounded June 14, 1863, at Port Hudson, La.

Priv. Thomas O'Halloran, Randolph; 27 years old; bootmaker; enlisted Sept. 17, 1862. Returned from Louisiana but died Aug. 26, 1863, at Mount Auburn, Mass.

Priv. Charles F. Packard, East Stoughton; 27 years old; bootmaker; enlisted Sept. 17, 1862. Died of disease March 29, 1863, at the General Hospital in Baton Rouge, La.

Priv. Adoniram A. Payne, Randolph; 29 years old; bootmaker; enlisted Sept. 17, 1862. Taken prisoner June 23, 1863, at Brashear City, La.

Priv. Zebulon S. Phillips, Randolph; 29 years old; bootmaker; enlisted Sept. 17, 1862. Taken prisoner June 23, 1863, at Brashear City, La.

Priv. David Pope, Randolph; 22 years old; bootmaker; enlisted Sept. 17, 1862. Taken prisoner June 23, 1863, at Brashear City, La.

Priv. Cyrus H. Porter, East Stoughton; 20 years old; farmer; enlisted Sept. 17, 1862.

Priv. Abram W. Pratt, Randolph; 30 years old; bootmaker; enlisted Sept. 17, 1862. Taken prisoner June 23, 1863, at Brashear City, La.

Priv. Martin Rogers, Randolph; 19 years old; boot fitter; enlisted Sept. 17, 1862. Discharged due to disability May 31, 1863, at Baton Rouge, La.

Priv. John Rooney, Randolph; 21 years old; bootmaker; enlisted Sept. 17, 1862.

Priv. Martin V. B. Shaw, Randolph; 26 years old; bootmaker; enlisted Sept. 17, 1862.

Priv. Elbridge G. Simpson, Randolph; 18 years old; farmer; enlisted Sept. 17, 1862. Died Aug. 30, 1863, in Randolph, Mass.

Priv. Henry Snow, Randolph; 21 years old; bootmaker; enlisted Sept. 17, 1862. Died Aug. 22, 1863, at the St. James Hospital in New Orleans, La.

Priv. William B. Spear, Randolph; 18 years old; boot cutter; enlisted Sept. 17, 1862.

Priv. Alvin H. Sprague, Randolph; 38 years old; boot fitter; enlisted Sept. 17, 1862. Taken prisoner June 23, 1863, at Brashear City, La.

Priv. Francis E. Stetson, Randolph; 18 years old; bootmaker; enlisted Sept. 17, 1862.

Priv. Patrick E. Sullivan, Randolph; 36 years old; boot cutter; enlisted Sept. 17, 1862.

Priv. Loring Taunt, Randolph; 28 years old; sailor; enlisted Sept. 17, 1862. Taken prisoner June 23, 1863, at Brashear City, La. Taunt must have reenlisted since Dargan notes in his diary that Taunt died in the Andersonville Prison.

Priv. Charles L. Thayer, Randolph; 34 years old; mason; enlisted Sept. 17, 1862. Thayer was a company bugler.

Priv. Charles Luther Thayer, Randolph; 20 years old; bootmaker; enlisted Sept. 17, 1862. Taken prisoner June 23, 1863, at Brashear City, La. Died Sept. 10, 1863, in Randolph, Mass.

Priv. Isaac Thayer, Jr., Randolph; 28 years old; boot cutter; enlisted Sept. 17, 1862. Also served in Company D, 4th Mass. Infantry for 3-month duty in 1861.

Priv. Leonard A. Thayer, Stoughton; 28 years old; boot cutter; enlisted Sept. 17, 1862.

Priv. Thomas B. Thayer, Randolph; 32 years old; boot cutter; enlisted Sept. 17, 1862.

Priv. Thomas H. B. Thayer, Randolph; 25 years old; boot fitter; enlisted Sept. 17, 1862.

Priv. Warren Thayer, Randolph; 21 years old; boot stitcher; enlisted Sept. 17, 1862.

Priv. John Tynan, Randolph; 26 years old; bootmaker; enlisted Sept. 17, 1862.

Priv. George Washburn, Randolph; 34 years old; boot cutter; enlisted Sept. 17, 1862. Taken prisoner June 23, 1863, at Brashear City, La. Died July 19, 1863, at the General Hospital in Brashear City, La.

Priv. Horace N. Wetherbee, Randolph; 23 years old; bootmaker; enlisted Sept. 17, 1862.

Priv. Martin P. Wetherbee, Randolph; 21 years old; butcher; enlisted Sept. 17, 1862.

Priv. James W. White, Randolph; 35 years old; boot fitter; enlisted Sept. 17, 1862. White played in the band.

Priv. Samuel White, Randolph; 31 years old; boot cutter; enlisted Sept. 17, 1862. Also played in the band.

Priv. William L. White, Randolph; 24 years old; teamster; enlisted Sept. 17, 1862. Taken prisoner June 23, 1863, at Brashear

City, La. Died Jan. 1864, in Randolph, Mass. Also served in Company D, 4th Mass. Infantry for 3-month duty in 1861.

COMPANY E

Captain Lewis Soule, South Abington; 28 years old; shoemaker; commissioned Sept. 22, 1862. Also served in Company E, 4th Mass. Infantry for 3-month duty in 1861.

1st Lieut. Henry Humble, Abington; 26 years old; shoemaker; commissioned Sept. 22, 1862. Taken prisoner June 23, 1863, at Brashear City, La. Also served in Company E, 4th Mass. Infantry for 3-month duty in 1861.

2d Lieut. John Maloy, South Abington; 41 years old; shoemaker; commissioned Sept. 22, 1862.

1st Sergt. William H. Maine, East Bridgewater; 24 years old; shoemaker; enlisted Sept. 23, 1862. Wounded June 14, 1863, at Port Hudson, La. Also served in Company E, 4th Mass. Infantry for 3-month duty in 1861.

Sergt. Morton E. Harding, Abington; 25 years old; painter; enlisted Sept. 23, 1862. Also served in Company E, 4th Mass. Infantry for 3-month duty in 1861.

Sergt. William R. Vining, South Abington; 37 years old; manufacturer; enlisted Sept. 23, 1862.

Sergt. Isaac Cook, South Abington; 34 years old; cutter; enlisted Sept. 23, 1862. Taken prisoner June 23, 1863, at Brashear City, La.

Sergt. John B. Hutchinson, South Abington; 40 years old; shoemaker; enlisted Sept. 23, 1862. Died of disease May 16, 1863, at Franklin, La.

Corpl. Lucius D. Burbeck, East Bridgewater; 38 years old; carpenter; enlisted Sept. 23, 1862.

Corpl. Alfred Sharp, South Abington; 35 years old; shoemaker; enlisted Sept. 23, 1862. Taken prisoner June 23, 1863, at Brashear City, La.

Corpl. Jacob P. Bates, South Abington; 19 years old; clerk; enlisted Sept. 23, 1862. Taken prisoner June 23, 1863, at Brashear City, La.

Corpl. Isaac R. French, East Bridgewater; 18 years old; shoemaker; enlisted Sept. 23, 1862.

Corpl. Gilbert Brown, East Bridgewater; 20 years old; shoemaker; enlisted Sept. 23, 1862.

Corpl. Wendell G. Corthell, South Abington; 18 years old; student; enlisted Sept. 23, 1862. Taken prisoner June 23, 1863, at Brashear City, La.

Corpl. Peter M. Leavitt, South Abington; 40 years old; cutter; enlisted Sept. 23, 1862. Taken prisoner June 23, 1863, at Brashear City, La.

Corpl. Josiah Richmond, East Bridgewater; 36 years old; farmer; enlisted Sept. 23, 1862. Left Louisiana in Aug. 1863 but died en route home on Aug. 15, 1863, at Marion, Ohio.

Music, John Brown, Hanson; 21 years old; nailer; enlisted Oct. 10, 1862.

Music, Howard A. Wheeler, Abington; 18 years old; student; enlisted Oct. 29, 1862.

Wagoner, Francis B. Chamberlin, East Bridgewater; 30 years old; peddler; enlisted Sept. 23, 1862.

Priv. Jared Alden, South Abington; 41 years old; farmer; enlisted Sept. 23, 1862. Discharged due to disability June 29, 1863.

Priv. John Alden, South Abington; 18 years old; shoemaker; enlisted Sept. 23, 1862.

Priv. Samuel S. Atwood, Abington; 29 years old; farmer; enlisted Sept. 23, 1862.

Priv. Solon Bates, South Abington; 21 years old; carpenter; enlisted Sept. 23, 1862. Died of disease May 29, 1863, in Brashear City, La.

Priv. William H. Bates, East Bridgewater; 20 years old; machinist; enlisted Sept. 23, 1862.

Priv. Josiah Beals, Abington; 24 years old; stitcher; enlisted Sept. 23, 1862.

Priv. Joseph F. Bisbee, Pembroke; 18 years old; farmer; enlisted Sept. 23, 1862.

Priv. Charles H. Bonney, East Bridgewater; 26 years old; carpenter; enlisted Sept. 23, 1862. Taken prisoner June 23, 1863, at Brashear City, La.

Priv. Henry L. Browne, Abington; 21 years old; stitcher; enlisted Sept. 23, 1862.

Priv. Michael Clark, South Abington; 41 years old; farmer; enlisted Sept. 23, 1862.

Priv. Albion Conant, Abington; 21 years old; cutter; enlisted Sept. 23, 1862.

Priv. Bartly Conroy, South Abington; 21 years old; shoemaker; enlisted Sept. 23, 1862. Taken prisoner June 23, 1863, at Brashear City, La.

Priv. James Conroy, South Abington; 38 years old; farmer; enlisted Sept. 23, 1862. Taken prisoner June 23, 1863, at Brashear City, La.

Priv. Luke Conroy, South Abington; 30 years old; shoemaker; enlisted Sept. 23, 1862.

Priv. Daniel Daley, Abington; 38 years old; laborer; enlisted Sept. 23, 1862. Died of disease June 16, 1863, at Brashear City, La.

Priv. Ichabod Deane, Easton; 44 years old; farmer; enlisted Sept. 23, 1862.

Priv. Henry F. Dunbar, North Bridgewater; 22 years old; shoemaker; enlisted Sept. 23, 1862. Taken prisoner June 23, 1863, at Brashear City, La. Also served in Company E, 4th Mass. Infantry for 3-month duty in 1861.

Priv. Volney H. Dunbar, Abington; 18 years old; shoemaker; enlisted Sept. 23, 1862.

Priv. Jason Duncan, South Abington; 19 years old; machinist; enlisted Sept. 23, 1862. Died of disease May 25, 1863, at Brashear City, La.

Priv. Wilson Ford, North Abington; 20 years old; shoemaker; enlisted Sept. 23, 1862.

Priv. Francis M. French, Abington; 29 years old; shoemaker; enlisted Sept. 23, 1862. Taken prisoner June 23, 1863, at Brashear City, La.

Priv. Thomas Galvian, South Abington; 23 years old; shoemaker; enlisted Sept. 23, 1862.

Priv. Cyrus J. Glover, Abington; 18 years old; shoemaker; enlisted Sept. 23, 1862. Taken prisoner June 23, 1863, at Brashear City, La.

Priv. Henry S. Green, Abington; 18 years old; occupation not given; enlisted Sept. 23, 1862. Discharged due to disability May 29, 1863.

Priv. Stephen Griggs, East Bridgewater; 23 years old; shoemaker; enlisted Sept. 23, 1862. Discharged due to disability May 4, 1863.

Priv. William Gurney, North Abington; 44 years old; shoemaker; enlisted Sept. 26, 1862.

Priv. Henry Z. Hale, East Bridgewater; 21 years old; shoemaker; enlisted Sept. 23, 1862.

Priv. Marcus M. Hale, East Bridgewater; 23 years old; shoemaker; enlisted Sept. 23, 1862.

Priv. Augustus F. Hall, East Bridgewater; 23 years old; shoemaker; enlisted Sept. 23, 1862.

Priv. Samuel Hall, East Bridgewater; 42 years old; carpenter; enlisted Sept. 23, 1862. Taken prisoner June 23, 1863, at Brashear City, La.

Priv. George G. Harding, South Abington; 28 years old; butcher; enlisted Sept. 23, 1862.

Priv. William H. Harding, South Abington; 24 years old; tacker; enlisted Sept. 23, 1862.

Priv. George E. Harrub, Plympton; 18 years old; shoemaker; enlisted Oct. 28, 1862. Died Aug. 8, 1863, aboard the steamer *North America.*

Priv. Edward Hayes, Abington; 29 years old; shoemaker; enlisted Sept. 23, 1862.

Priv. Charles M. Howard, Abington; 18 years old; shoemaker; enlisted Sept. 23, 1862.

Priv. Ward Hunt, Abington; 22 years old; stitcher; enlisted Sept. 23, 1862.

Priv. William Jones, South Abington; 42 years old; shoemaker; enlisted Sept. 23, 1862.

Priv. James Keran, Abington; 35 years old; shoemaker; enlisted Sept. 23, 1862.

Priv. Abel T. Lewis, Duxbury; 19 years old; shoemaker; enlisted Oct. 28, 1862. Died of disease June 26, 1863, in New Orleans, La.

Priv. James P. Lincoln, Abington; 41 years old; shoemaker; enlisted Sept. 23, 1862.

Priv. William W. Lincoln, Abington; 18 years old; shoemaker; enlisted Sept. 23, 1862.

Priv. George Longley, North Abington; 40 years old; farmer; enlisted Sept. 23, 1862. Discharged due to disability Jan. 6, 1863.

Priv. Frank Longreen, Abington; 26 years old; farmer; enlisted Sept. 23, 1862.

Priv. Michael Luddy, Abington; 30 years old; treer; enlisted Sept. 26, 1862. Died of disease Aug. 14, 1863, at Port Hudson, La.

Priv. Lawrence McGoff, Hanson; 38 years old; farmer; enlisted Sept. 23, 1862.

Priv. Charles A. Millett, South Abington; 18 years old; shoemaker; enlisted Sept. 23, 1862.

Priv. George A. Morse, South Abington; 32 years old; shoemaker; enlisted Sept. 23, 1862.

Priv. Merrit Noyes, Abington; 20 years old; clerk; enlisted Sept. 23, 1862. Wounded June 14, 1863, at Port Hudson, La.

Priv. John Parmenter, Abington; 30 years old; shoemaker; enlisted Sept. 23, 1862. Taken prisoner June 23, 1863, at Brashear City, La.

Priv. George H. Pearson, South Abington; 24 years old; clerk; enlisted Sept. 23, 1862. Taken prisoner June 23, 1863, at Brashear City, La.

Priv. Albert S. Peck, North Bridgewater; 21 years old; blacksmith; enlisted Sept. 23, 1862.

Priv. George E. Peck, Swansea; 27 years old; painter; enlisted Oct. 17, 1862.

Priv. Lewis P. Penniman, Abington; 22 years old; shoemaker; enlisted Sept. 23, 1862.

Priv. Aaron Alden Reed, South Abington; 23 years old; shoemaker; enlisted Sept. 23, 1862.

Priv. Clinton W. Reed, South Abington; 20 years old; shoe cutter; enlisted Sept. 23, 1862. Taken prisoner June 23, 1863, at Brashear City, La.

Priv. Cyrus Reed, South Abington; 27 years old; shoemaker; enlisted Sept. 23, 1862. Discharged due to disability May 22, 1863.

Priv. William H. Robbins, Abington; 18 years old; shoemaker; enlisted Sept. 23, 1862. Died of disease June 7, 1863, in Baton Rouge, La.

Priv. William Ryan, South Abington; 38 years old; laborer; enlisted Sept. 23, 1862. Discharged due to disability Jan. 6, 1863.

Priv. Oliver M. Sharp, East Bridgewater; 26 years old; shoemaker; enlisted Sept. 22, 1862.

Priv. Charles Shaw, II, Abington; 21 years old; stitcher; enlisted Sept. 23, 1862. Returned from Louisiana but died en route Aug. 31, 1863, at Rochester, N.Y.

Priv. Charles F. Shaw, East Bridgewater; 37 years old; shoemaker; enlisted Sept. 23, 1862. Returned from Louisiana but died en route Aug. 9, 1863, on board the steamer *North America*.

Priv. Winslow B. Sherman, Plymouth; 42 years old; laborer; enlisted Oct. 29, 1862. Transferred to Company C, March 1, 1863.

Priv. Jacob P. Spooner, East Bridgewater; 27 years old; mechanic; enlisted Sept. 23, 1862.

Priv. John W. Sproul, South Abington; 18 years old, tailor; enlisted Sept. 23, 1862.

Priv. Jason E. Stetson, East Bridgewater; 20 years old; carpenter; enlisted Sept. 23, 1862.

Priv. John M. Stetson, East Bridgewater; 27 years old; shoemaker; enlisted Sept. 23, 1862. Taken prisoner June 23, 1863, at Brashear City, La.

Priv. John Sullivan, Abington; 21 years old; tack maker; enlisted Sept. 23, 1862. Died of disease June 26, 1863, at Brashear City, La.

Priv. Jeremiah D. Thurlow, East Bridgewater; 35 years old; shoemaker; enlisted Sept. 23, 1862.

Priv. Henry Washburn, Kingston; 18 years old; shoemaker; enlisted Sept. 23, 1862.

Priv. Henry M. West, South Abington; 31 years old; carpenter; enlisted Sept. 23, 1862.

Priv. George F. Wheeler, Abington; 44 years old; hotel keeper; enlisted Oct. 29, 1862. Taken prisoner June 23, 1863, at Brashear City, La.

Priv. Charles H. W. Whiting, 18 years old; shoemaker; enlisted Sept. 23, 1862.

Priv. Thomas A. Whitmarsh, South Abington; 19 years old; shoemaker; enlisted Sept. 23, 1862.

Priv. George H. Wright, South Abington; 18 years old; mechanic; enlisted Sept. 23, 1862.

Company F

Captain William R. Black, Taunton; 33 years old; carpenter; commissioned Dec. 15, 1862. Originally 1st Lieut. of Company G. Also served in Company G, 4th Mass. Infantry for 3-month duty in 1861.

1st Lieut. Moses A. Richardson, Foxboro; 38 years old; occupation not given; commissioned Sept. 10, 1862. Resigned Sept. 23, 1862. Also served in Company F, 4th Mass. Infantry for 3-month duty in 1861.

1st Lieut. Benjamin H. Richmond, Norton; 41 years old; boot manufacturer; commissioned Dec. 18, 1862.

2d Lieut. Isaac H. Bonney, Foxboro; 20 years old; student; commissioned Dec. 18, 1862. Returned from Louisiana but died en route Aug. 23, 1863, at Indianapolis, Ind. Also served in Company F, 4th Mass. Infantry for 3-month duty in 1861.

1st Sergt. Joseph H. Joplin, Foxboro; 23 years old; bootmaker; enlisted Sept. 19, 1862. Returned from Louisiana but died en route Aug. 15, 1863, on the Illinois Central Railroad between Cairo and Mattoon. Also served in Company F, 4th Mass. Infantry for 3-month duty in 1861.

Sergt. Horatio W. Caswell, Raynham; 22 years old; shovel maker; enlisted Sept. 19, 1862.

Sergt. Emery E. Willis, Norton; 29 years old; moulder; enlisted Sept. 19, 1862.

Sergt. Liscomb C. Winn, Foxboro; 19 years old; hat blocker; enlisted Sept. 19, 1862. Also served in Company F, 4th Mass. Infantry for 3-month duty in 1861.

Sergt. Lewis H. Sweet, Norton; 24 years old; teacher; enlisted Sept. 19, 1862. Died June 15, 1863, at University Hospital, New Orleans, La., from wounds received on June 14, 1863, at Port Hudson, La.

Sergt. Gabriel P. Chamberlain, Foxboro; 25 years old; bonnet presser; enlisted Sept. 19, 1862. Died of disease May 31, 1863, at Brashear City, La. Also served in Company F, 4th Mass. Infantry for 3-month duty in 1861.

Corpl. Ephraim O. Grover, Foxboro; 27 years old; bonnet presser; enlisted Sept. 19, 1862. Taken prisoner June 23, 1863, at Brashear City, La. Also served in Company F, 4th Mass. Infantry for 3-month duty in 1861.

Corpl. Paschal C. Grover, Foxboro; 23 years old; clerk; enlisted Sept. 19, 1862. Taken prisoner June 23, 1863, at Brashear City, La. Also served in Company F, 4th Mass. Infantry for 3-month duty in 1861.

Corpl. Charles B. Winn, Foxboro; 22 years old; bonnet packer; enlisted Sept. 19, 1862.

Corpl. Charles W. Sprague, Norton; 28 years old; machinist; enlisted Sept. 19, 1862.

Corpl. Henry L. Pratt, Raynham; 29 years old; nailer; enlisted Sept. 19, 1862.

Corpl. Charles T. Sumner, Foxboro; 28 years old; bonnet presser; enlisted Sept. 19, 1862. Taken prisoner June 23, 1863, at Brashear City, La.

Corpl. Derick W. Cobb, Norton; 20 years old; jeweller; enlisted Sept. 19, 1862. Died of disease Jan. 21, 1863, at General Hospital, New York City, N.Y.

Music George H. Grover, Foxboro; 16 years old; student; enlisted Sept. 19, 1862.

Music William M. Adams, Foxboro; 45 years old; farmer; enlisted Sept. 19, 1862. Died of disease March 6, 1863, at the regimental hospital in New Carrollton, La.

Wagoner Artemas C. King, Jr., Norton; 28 years old; jeweller; enlisted Sept. 19, 1862.

Priv. Joseph H. Alden, Foxboro; 19 years old; printer; enlisted Sept. 19, 1862.

Priv. Warren B. Alden, Foxboro; 44 years old; bonnet presser; enlisted Sept. 19, 1862. Discharged due to disability Dec. 8, 1862.

Priv. Albert A. Austin, Norton; 18 years old; farmer; enlisted Sept. 19, 1862. Wounded June 14, 1863, at Port Hudson, La.

Priv. Granville D. Austin, Norton; 18 years old; farmer; enlisted Sept. 19, 1862.

Priv. Lewis W. Belcher, Foxboro; 36 years old; butcher; enlisted Sept. 19, 1862.

Priv. Abbott H. Blandin, Norton; 18 years old; bootmaker; enlisted Sept. 19, 1862.

Priv. William S. Bolton, Norton; 32 years old; farmer; enlisted Sept. 19, 1862. Died of disease June 26, 1863, at Brashear City, La.

Priv. Charles L. Boyden, Foxboro; 19 years old; bootmaker; enlisted Oct. 15, 1862. Died July 15, 1863, at New Orleans, La., from wounds received June 14, 1863, at Port Hudson, La.

Priv. Edwin J. Carroll, Foxboro; 18 years old; student; enlisted Sept. 19, 1862. Wounded June 14, 1863, at Port Hudson, La.

Priv. James S. Carver, Foxboro; 22 years old; hat blocker; enlisted Sept. 19, 1862.

Priv. Elijah Caswell, Jr., Raynham; 29 years old; shovel maker; enlisted Sept. 19, 1862.

Priv. George H. Copliston, Foxboro; 25 years old; bonnet presser; enlisted Sept. 19, 1862. Taken prisoner June 23, 1863, at Brashear City, La.

Priv. William Day, Foxboro; 32 years old; hat blocker; enlisted Sept. 19, 1862. Died of disease June 10, 1863, at Brashear City, La.

Priv. Robert Dixon, Norton; 37 years old; farmer; enlisted Sept. 19, 1862. Discharged due to disability Dec. 18, 1862, at Boston, Mass.

Priv. Francis L. Dow, Raynham; 22 years old; nailer; enlisted Sept. 19, 1862.

Priv. Joseph H. Dow, Foxboro; 19 years old; sailor; enlisted Sept. 19, 1862.

Priv. Edwin Dunbar, Foxboro; 34 years old; block maker; enlisted Sept. 19, 1862.

Priv. Darius B. Field, Norton; 37 years old; farmer; enlisted Sept. 19, 1862.

Priv. Anson Fisher, Foxboro; 30 years old; bonnet bleacher; enlisted Sept. 19, 1862. Wounded June 14, 1863, at Port Hudson, La.

Priv. E. Irving Fisher, Foxboro; 24 years old; bonnet presser; enlisted Sept. 19, 1862.

Priv. George H. Fisher, Foxboro; 19 years old; harness maker; enlisted Oct. 16, 1862.

Priv. Handel P. Fisher, Foxboro; 18 years old; farmer; enlisted Sept. 19, 1862.

Priv. Carlos D. Freeman, Foxboro; 21 years old; farmer; enlisted Sept. 19, 1862. Wounded June 14, 1863, at Port

Hudson, La., and died from the wounds and disease July 17, 1863, at Baton Rouge, La.

Priv. Edward M. Freeman, Foxboro; 24 years old; bootmaker; enlisted Sept. 19, 1862. Also served in Company F, 4th Mass. Infantry for 3-month duty in 1861.

Priv. William Gilchrist, Raynham; 35 years old; farmer; enlisted Sept. 19, 1862. Taken prisoner June 23, 1863, at Brashear City, La.

Priv. Bennajah W. Hathaway, Raynham; 28 years old; nailer; enlisted Sept. 19, 1862.

Priv. Alfred B. Hodges, Norton; 22 years old; clerk; enlisted Sept. 19, 1862.

Priv. David L. Hodges, Norton; 20 years old; clerk; enlisted Oct. 15, 1862. Wounded June 14, 1863, at Port Hudson, La.

Priv. Henry B. Ide, Norton; 18 years old; farmer; enlisted Sept. 19, 1862.

Priv. George S. Jones, Falmouth; 22 years old; student; enlisted Sept. 19, 1862.

Priv. Theodore W. Keith, Norton; 19 years old; farmer; enlisted Sept. 19, 1862. Died of disease July 20, 1863, at Barracks U.S. General Hospital in New Orleans, La.

Priv. William A. Lane, Norton; 21 years old; farmer; enlisted Sept. 19, 1862. Discharged due to disability April 9, 1863, at Boston, Mass.

Priv. Joseph Lincoln, Norton; 25 years old; farmer; enlisted Sept. 19, 1862. Wounded June 14, 1863, at Port Hudson, La., and died from his wounds July 3, 1863, at Brashear City, La.

Priv. Zacheus Macomber, Norton; 45 years old; blacksmith; enlisted Sept. 19, 1862. Died of disease Jan. 24, 1863, on board the steamer *Continental*.

Priv. George A. Mann, Foxboro; 22 years old; bonnet presser; enlisted Sept. 19, 1862.

Priv. Cyrus B. Morse, Foxboro; 20 years old; box maker; enlisted Sept. 19, 1862.

Priv. Elbridge F. Morse, Foxboro; 25 years old; farmer; enlisted Sept. 19, 1862. Died of disease May 26, 1863, at New Orleans, La.

Priv. Jairus J. Morse, Foxboro; 20 years old; farmer; enlisted Sept. 19, 1862.

Priv. William A. Morse, Foxboro; 18 years old; baker; enlisted Sept. 19, 1862. Also served in Company F, 4th Mass. Infantry for 3-month duty in 1861.

Priv. Joseph Myers, Foxboro; 22 years old; basket maker; enlisted Sept. 19, 1862. Taken prisoner June 23, 1863, at Brashear City, La., and died July 20, 1863, at New Orleans, La.

Priv. Charles A. Pettee, Foxboro; 18 years old; student; enlisted Sept. 19, 1862.

Priv. Samuel Phillips, Raynham; 23 years old; nailer; enlisted Sept. 19, 1862.

Priv. Bernard L. Ripley, Norton; 21 years old; farmer; enlisted Sept. 19, 1862. Died of disease June 22, 1863, at Baton Rouge, La.

Priv. Henry Sherman, Norton; 45 years old; dresser; enlisted Sept. 19, 1862.

Priv. Charles D. Smith, Foxboro; 34 years old; bootmaker; enlisted Sept. 19, 1862.

Priv. Charles T. Smith, Norton; 29 years old; farmer; enlisted Sept. 19, 1862.

Priv. Leonard Smith, Foxboro; 25 years old; painter; enlisted Sept. 19, 1862.

Priv. Payson F. Smith, Foxboro; 19 years old; baker; enlisted Sept. 19, 1862.

Priv. William A. Stephens, Foxboro; 30 years old; carpenter; enlisted Sept. 19, 1862.

Priv. Henry C. Sumner, Foxboro; 19 years old; bonnet blocker; enlisted Sept. 19, 1862. Returned from Louisiana but died en route Aug. 13, 1863, on the Illinois Central Railroad between Cairo and Mattoon.

Priv. Cyril S. Sweet, Norton; 45 years old; ice dealer; enlisted Sept. 19, 1862. Discharged due to disability March 28, 1863, at Boston, Mass.

Priv. David A. Swift, Foxboro; 24 years old; trader; enlisted Sept. 19, 1862.

Priv. Charles A. Thompson, Foxboro; 29 years old; bonnet presser; enlisted Oct. 15, 1862. Also served in Company F, 4th Mass. Infantry for 3-month duty in 1861.

Priv. George S. Thompson, Foxboro; 20 years old; bonnet presser; enlisted Sept. 19, 1862.

Priv. Henry O. Titus, Norton; 25 years old; bootmaker; enlisted Sept. 19, 1862. Died of disease Feb. 17, 1863, in the Regimental Hospital, Carrollton, La.

Priv. George N. Tucker, Norton; 23 years old; mason; enlisted Sept. 19, 1862. Died of disease March 2, 1863, in the Regimental Hospital, Carrollton, La.

Priv. John Ware, Foxboro; 18 years old; blacksmith; enlisted Sept. 19, 1862.

Priv. Alexander D. Washburn, Norton; 20 years old; farmer; enlisted Sept. 19, 1862.

Priv. Charles H. Wetherell, Norton; 22 years old; farmer; enlisted Sept. 19, 1862.

Priv. Thomas B. Wetherell, Norton; 24 years old; carpenter; enlisted Sept. 19, 1862. Discharged due to disability April 6, 1863, at Boston, Mass.

Priv. Calvin White, Norton; 23 years old; bootmaker; enlisted Sept. 19, 1862. Taken prisoner June 23, 1863, at Brashear City, La.

Priv. Jason White, Norton; 45 years old; music teacher; enlisted Sept. 19, 1862. Taken prisoner June 23, 1863, at Brashear City, La.

Priv. John H. White, Norton; 32 years old; bootmaker; enlisted Sept. 19, 1862.

Priv. Preston B. Whittemore, Foxboro; 37 years old; undertaker; enlisted Sept. 19, 1862.

Priv. James Wight, Foxboro; 32 years old; farmer; enlisted Sept. 19, 1862. Taken prisoner June 23, 1863, at Brashear City, La.

Priv. Ansel L. Willis, Foxboro; 26 years old; farmer; enlisted Sept. 19, 1862.

Priv. Loren B. Willis, Norton; 21 years old; farmer; enlisted Sept. 19, 1862.

COMPANY G

Captain Charles H. Paull, Taunton; 32 years old; merchant; commissioned Aug. 27, 1862. Also served in Company G, 4th Mass. Infantry for 3-month duty in 1861.

1st Lieut. William R. Black, Taunton; 33 years old, carpenter; commissioned Aug. 27, 1862. Commissioned captain, Company F, Dec. 15, 1862.

1st Lieut. William J. Briggs, Taunton; 39 years old; mason; commissioned Dec. 18, 1862. Also served in Company G, 4th Mass. Infantry for 3-month duty in 1861.

2d Lieut. William H. Monroe, Taunton; 23 years old; spinner; enlisted Sept. 15, 1862; commissioned Dec. 18, 1862. Also served in Company G, 4th Mass. Infantry for 3-month duty in 1861.

1st Sergt. Lewis B. Hodges, Taunton; 28 years old; moulder; enlisted Sept. 15, 1862. Promoted to 1st Sergt., Dec. 18, 1862.

Sergt. George Murray, Taunton; 38 years old; machinist; enlisted Sept. 15, 1862.

Sergt. Ansel Balcom, Jr., Taunton; 28 years old; restauranteur; enlisted Sept. 15, 1862.

Sergt. Henry A. Paull, Taunton; 23 years old; merchant; enlisted Sept. 15, 1862.

Sergt. James L. Tisdale, Taunton; 39 years old; farmer; enlisted Sept. 15, 1862. Died en route home Aug. 13, 1863, on board the steamer *Pioneer*.

Corpl. Lemuel C. Porter, Taunton; 24 years old; brittannia worker; enlisted Sept. 15, 1862. Taken prisoner June 23, 1863, at Brashear City, La.

Corpl. William L. Walker, Taunton; 22 years old; farmer; enlisted Sept. 15, 1862. Wounded June 14, 1863, at Port Hudson, La.

Corpl. Thomas C. Brown, Taunton; 24 years old; tailor; enlisted Sept. 15, 1862. Died of disease Aug. 17, 1863, at the General Hospital in Baton Rouge, La.

Corpl. Laughlin Walsh, Taunton; 30 years old; carpenter; enlisted Sept. 15, 1862.

Corpl. Charles H. Briggs, Dighton; 34 years old; farmer; enlisted Sept. 15, 1862.

Corpl. Jeremiah C. Turner, Taunton; 28 years old; printer; enlisted Sept. 15, 1862. Taken prisoner June 23, 1863, at Brashear City, La.

Corpl. Lorenzo O. Barnard, Taunton; 30 years old; occupation not given; enlisted Sept. 15, 1862. Taken prisoner June 23, 1863, at Brashear City, La.

Corpl. James L. Presbrey, Taunton; 33 years old; carpenter; enlisted Sept. 15, 1862.

Music William H. Paine, Taunton; 18 years old; occupation not given; enlisted Dec. 18, 1862.

Music Charles H. Gibbs, Taunton; 22 years old; painter; enlisted Sept. 15, 1862.

Wagoner Horatio Raymond, Taunton; 31 years old; teamster; enlisted Sept. 15, 1862. Discharged due to disability Jan. 14, 1863.

Priv. William B. Allyn, Taunton; 22 years old; clerk; enlisted Sept. 15, 1862. Taken prisoner June 23, 1863, at Brashear City, La.

Priv. Luther G. Ashley, Taunton; 30 years old; mason; enlisted Sept. 15, 1862.

Priv. Alden H. Blake, Taunton; 27 years old; carpenter; enlisted Sept. 15, 1862.

Priv. Thomas Bliss, Rehoboth; 22 years old; framer; enlisted Sept. 15, 1862. Died of disease May 18, 1863, in the General Hospital, Berwick City, La.

Priv. Francis T. Burns, Taunton; 20 years old; moulder; enlisted Sept. 15, 1862. Taken prisoner June 23, 1863, at Brashear City, La.

Priv. Jerome B. Burt, Taunton; 20 years old; moulder; enlisted Sept. 15, 1862. Died of disease June 11, 1863, in the General Hospital, Brashear City, La.

Priv. James Butler, Taunton; 24 years old; barber; enlisted Sept. 22, 1862.

Priv. Hiram T. Cain, Raynham; 21 years old; shoe cutter; enlisted Sept. 29, 1862. Taken prisoner June 23, 1863, Brashear City, La.

Priv. Isaac H. Carpenter, Rehoboth; 21 years old; brittannia worker; enlisted Sept. 15, 1862.

Priv. William B. Carpenter, Taunton; 20 years old; machinist; enlisted Sept. 15, 1862.

Priv. William H. Case, Taunton; 20 years old; clerk; enlisted Sept. 15, 1862.

Priv. Sylvester J. Clement, Taunton; 30 years old; blacksmith; enlisted Sept. 15, 1862.

Priv. Benjamin O. Colwell, Taunton; 22 years old; clerk; enlisted Sept. 15, 1862.

Priv. John Conaty, Taunton; 23 years old; machinist; enlisted Sept. 15, 1862.

Priv. Daniel A. Congdon, Taunton; 19 years old; clerk; enlisted Sept. 15, 1862. Taken prisoner June 23, 1863, at Brashear City, La.

Priv. Levi K. Congdon, Taunton; 19 years old; machinist; enlisted Sept. 15, 1862.

Priv. George A. Crane, Taunton; 26 years old; farmer; enlisted Sept. 15, 1862.

Priv. John Cunningham, Taunton; 24 years old; moulder; enlisted Sept. 22, 1862.

Priv. Charles W. Dean, Taunton; 19 years old; nailer; enlisted Sept. 15, 1862.

Priv. Edward B. Durfee, Taunton; 23 years old; clerk; enlisted Sept. 15, 1862. Taken prisoner June 23, 1863, at Brashear City, La.

Priv. Marcus M. Field, Taunton; 24 years old; brittannia worker; enlisted Sept. 15, 1862. Taken prisoner June 23, 1863, at Brashear City, La.

Priv. Elijah D. Goddard, Taunton; 21 years old; brittannia worker; enlisted Sept. 15, 1862. Also served in Company G, 4th Mass. Infantry for 3-month duty in 1861.

Priv. Seth W. Godfrey, Taunton; 20 years old; carriage maker; enlisted Sept. 15, 1862.

Priv. James W. Gulliver, Taunton; 20 years old; farmer; enlisted Sept. 15, 1862. Died of disease April 3, 1863, in the General Hospital, Baton Rouge, La.

Priv. Samuel M. Gushee, Taunton; 19 years old; carpenter; enlisted Sept. 15, 1862. Taken prisoner June 23, 1863, at Brashear City, La.

Priv. George B. Harvey, Taunton; 22 years old; shoemaker; enlisted Sept. 15, 1862. Taken prisoner June 23, 1863, at Brashear City, La.

Priv. Oscar A. Harvey, Taunton; 20 years old; moulder; enlisted Sept. 15, 1862. Died of disease Feb. 15, 1863, in Louisiana (city not noted).

Priv. Laban Hodges, Taunton; 22 years old; butcher; enlisted Sept. 15, 1862.

Priv. Patrick Hogan, Taunton; 35 years old; blacksmith; enlisted Sept. 15, 1862.

Priv. Isaac H. Howland, Taunton; 23 years old; brickmaker; enlisted Sept. 15, 1862.

Priv. Albert H. Hunter, Taunton; 20 years old; machinist; enlisted Sept. 15, 1862.

Priv. Marcus E. Jones, Taunton; 24 years old; hostler; enlisted Sept. 15, 1862.

Priv. Timothy J. Lincoln, Raynham; 24 years old; farmer; enlisted Sept. 15, 1862. Taken prisoner June 23, 1863, at Brashear City, La.

Priv. Timothy C. Lucas, Taunton; 26 years old; blacksmith; enlisted Sept. 15, 1862.

Priv. Edward F. Macomber, Taunton; 24 years old; brickmaker; enlisted Sept. 15, 1862.

Priv. George A. Macomber, Taunton; 30 years old; carpenter; enlisted Sept. 15, 1862.

Priv. William E. Macomber, Taunton; 27 years old; carpenter; enlisted Sept. 15, 1862.

Priv. William F. Macomber, Jr., Taunton; 23 years old; brickmaker; enlisted Sept. 15, 1862. Died July 20, 1863, Ship Island, Miss.

Priv. George R. Marshall, Taunton; 21 years old; machinist; enlisted Sept. 15, 1862.

Priv. Henry Martin, Taunton; 23 years old; carpenter; enlisted Sept. 15, 1862.

Priv. John L. Merigold, Taunton; 23 years old; clerk; enlisted Sept. 15, 1862. Also served in Company G, 4th Mass. Infantry for 3-month duty in 1861.

Priv. George M. Nichols, Taunton; 30 years old; fish merchant; enlisted Sept. 15, 1862. Taken prisoner June 23, 1863, at Brashear City, La.

Priv. William D. Packard, Taunton; 25 years old; machinist; enlisted Sept. 15, 1862. Taken prisoner June 23, 1863, at Brasher City, La.

Priv. Lyman Palmer, Taunton; 22 years old; carder; enlisted Sept. 29, 1862.

Priv. George W. Peck, Taunton; 19 years old; butcher; enlisted Sept. 15, 1862.

Priv. Henry C. Phillips, Taunton; 25 years old; machinist; enlisted Sept. 15, 1862. Died of disease June 2, 1863, at the General Hospital in Brashear City, La.

Priv. Andrew W. Pierce, Taunton; 23 years old; clerk; enlisted Sept. 15, 1862.

Priv. Willis S. Potter, Taunton; 19 years old; blacksmith; enlisted Sept. 15, 1862. Wounded June 14, 1863, at Port Hudson, La.

Priv. Enos A. Pratt, Taunton; 23 years old; butcher; enlisted Sept. 15, 1862.

Priv. William B. Pratt, Taunton; 20 years old; farmer; enlisted Sept. 15, 1862. Died Jan. 9, 1863, on board the *George Peabody* in Hampton Roads, Va.

Priv. Edwin F. Presbrey, Taunton; 40 years old; engineer; enlisted Sept. 15, 1862.

Priv. Josiah E. Presbrey, Taunton; 44 years old; cotton manufacturer; enlisted Sept. 22, 1862. Taken prisoner June 23, 1863, at Brashear City, La.

Priv. Albert F. Smith, Taunton; 21 years old; brittannia worker; enlisted Sept. 15, 1862. Left Louisiana but died en route Aug. 12, 1863, at Cairo, Ill.

Priv. Andrew J. Smith, Taunton; 21 years old; blacksmith; enlisted Sept. 15, 1862.

Priv. William H. Stall, Taunton; 28 years old; carpenter; enlisted Sept. 15, 1862. Killed in action June 23, 1863, at Brashear City, La.

Priv. Edwin S. Thayer, Taunton; 20 years old; farmer; enlisted Sept. 22, 1862.

Priv. Josiah A. Tilden, Taunton; 25 years old; clerk; enlisted Sept. 15, 1862.

Priv. James A. Tinkham, Taunton; 20 years old; clerk; enlisted Sept. 15, 1862.

Priv. Edward E. Tisdale, Taunton; 19 years old; moulder; enlisted Sept. 15, 1862. Taken prisoner June 23, 1863, at Brashear City, La.

Priv. Franklin D. Tripp, Taunton; 23 years old; brass finisher; enlisted Sept. 15, 1862.

Priv. George Waldron, Taunton; 26 years old; tack maker; enlisted Sept. 15, 1862. Taken prisoner June 23, 1863, at Brashear City, La.

Priv. Daniel B. Walker, Taunton; 25 years old; surveyor; enlisted Sept. 15, 1862.

Priv. Edsell H. Walker, Taunton; 29 years old; laborer; enlisted Sept. 15, 1862. Died of disease May 11, 1863, in Berwick City, La.

Priv. Elnathan Walker, II, Taunton; 29 years old; farmer; enlisted Sept. 15, 1862.

Priv. Joseph Walker, II, Taunton; 32 years old; moulder; enlisted Sept. 15, 1862. Discharged due to disability May 5, 1863. Also served in Company G, 4th Mass. Infantry for 3-month duty in 1861.

Priv. Frederick A. Washburn, Taunton; 24 years old; undertaker; enlisted Sept. 15, 1862. Also served in Company G, 4th Mass. Infantry for 3-month duty in 1861.

Priv. William Watts, Taunton; 28 years old; painter; enlisted Sept. 15, 1862.

Priv. Alexander White, Taunton; 20 years old; farmer; enlisted Sept. 15, 1862.

Priv. Charles P. White, Taunton; 19 years old; moulder; enlisted Sept. 15, 1862.

Priv. George E. Wilbur, Taunton; 19 years old; machinist; enlisted Sept. 15, 1862.

Priv. Joseph W. Wilbur, Raynham; 23 years old; blacksmith; enlisted Sept. 15, 1862.

Priv. Joseph H. Wilcox, Taunton; 21 years old; engineer; enlisted Sept. 15, 1862.

Priv. George F. Williams, Taunton; 23 years old; farmer; enlisted Sept. 15, 1862.

Priv. Lemuel Allen Williams, Taunton; 23 years old; sailor; enlisted Nov. 5, 1862.

Priv. Henry P. Worsley, Taunton; 20 years old; machinist; enlisted Sept. 15, 1862.

COMPANY H

Captain John R. Rollins, Lawrence; 45 years old; clerk; commissioned Sept. 9, 1862.

1st Lieut. James G. Abbott, Lawrence; 26 years old; expressman; commissioned Sept. 9, 1862.

2d Lieut. Hiram Robinson, Lawrence; 24 years old; grocer; commissioned Sept. 9, 1862.

1st Sergt. John F. Benson, Lawrence; 28 years old; weaver; enlisted Aug. 28, 1862. Taken prisoner June 23, 1863, at Brashear City, La.

Sergt. Charles W. Butler, Lawrence; 36 years old; painter; enlisted Aug. 30, 1862.

Sergt. Thomas P. Kemp, Lawrence; 25 years old; operative; enlisted Aug. 29, 1862.

Sergt. Milo J. Chapin, Lawrence; 33 years old; trader; enlisted Sept. 4, 1862. Taken prisoner June 23, 1863, at Brashear City, La.

Sergt. Elbridge E. Hosmer, Lawrence; 21 years old; carpenter; enlisted Aug. 30, 1862. Taken prisoner June 23, 1863, at Brashear City, La.

Sergt. Carlton Kimball, Lawrence; 27 years old; merchant; enlisted Aug. 30, 1862. Discharged Nov. 21, 1862, due to disability at Camp Wenham, Mass.

Corpl. Joseph Scofield, Lawrence; 33 years old; trader; enlisted Sept. 12, 1862.

Corpl. John Roberts, Lawrence; 45 years old; cloth finisher; enlisted Aug. 30, 1862.

Corpl. Gilman P. Wiggin, Lawrence; 23 years old; merchant; enlisted Aug. 28, 1862.

Corpl. William C. Lyle, Lawrence; 44 years old; calico printer; enlisted Sept. 20, 1862.

Corpl. Charles G. Kimball, Bradford; 30 years old; stable keeper; enlisted Aug. 30, 1862.

Corpl. William H. Wells, Lawrence; 27 years old; painter; enlisted Sept. 4, 1862.

Corpl. James L. Davis, Lawrence; 18 years old; tailor; enlisted Aug. 30, 1862.

Corpl. Chase C. French, Lawrence; 38 years old; hostler; enlisted Aug. 28, 1862. Died Aug. 1, 1863, of disease at Port Hudson, La.

Music Joshua C. Merrow, Lawrence; 45 years old; carpenter; enlisted Aug. 28, 1862. Taken prisoner June 23, 1863, at Brashear City, La.

Wagoner Horatio R. Mudgett, Lawrence; 26 years old; butcher; enlisted Aug. 28, 1862. Discharged Dec. 17, 1862, due to disability.

Wagoner Thomas Mudgett, Lawrence; 45 years old; teamster; enlisted Sept. 24, 1862.

Priv. Charles Alison, Lawrence; 24 years old; farmer; enlisted Sept. 30, 1862. Died April 16, 1863, of disease at Baton Rouge, La.

Priv. Joseph Babb, Lawrence; 18 years old; spinner; enlisted Aug. 29, 1862.

Priv. James Barry, Lawrence; 23 years old; finisher; enlisted Aug. 30, 1862. Wounded June 14, 1863, at Port Hudson, La.

Priv. Bodwell D. Beadle, Lawrence; 35 years old; painter; enlisted Aug. 29, 1862.

Priv. George Bennett, Lawrence; 38 years old; operative; enlisted Sept. 3, 1862.

Priv. James Bingham, Lawrence; 22 years old; finisher, enlisted Aug. 28, 1862. Died April 25, 1863, of disease at Baton Rouge, La.

Priv. James P. Brown, Lawrence; 19 years old; operative; enlisted Sept. 30, 1862.

Priv. Austin Butler, Lawrence; 18 years old; operative; enlisted Sept. 2, 1862.

Priv. Coleman Butler, Lawrence; 27 years old; operative; enlisted Sept. 1, 1862.

Priv. Thomas Callahan, Lawrence; 38 years old; dyer; enlisted Aug. 28, 1862.

Priv. Duncan Campbell, Lawrence; 43 years old; dyer; enlisted Aug. 27, 1862. Wounded June 14, 1863, at Port Hudson, La.

Priv. John Casey, Lawrence; 18 years old; operative; enlisted Aug. 29, 1862.

Priv. Fitz Henry Chadwick, Lawrence; 22 years old; clerk; enlisted Sept. 6, 1862.

Priv. Edward H. Clarendon, Lawrence; 21 years old; sailor; enlisted Aug. 29, 1862.

Priv. Patrick Cline, Lawrence; 34 years old; peddler, enlisted Sept. 23, 1862.

Priv. Timothy Collins, Lawrence; 18 years old; dyer; enlisted Aug. 29, 1862.

Priv. James H. Conant, Lawrence; 18 years old; carpenter; enlisted Sept. 15, 1862.

Priv. John Condon, Lawrence; 25 years old; laborer; enlisted Sept. 15, 1862.

Priv. Benjamin C. Cook, Lawrence; 18 years old; clerk; enlisted Sept. 1, 1862.

Priv. Charles Cosanick, Lawrence; 38 years old; shoemaker; enlisted Sept. 18, 1862. Wounded June 14, 1863, at Port Hudson, La.

Priv. Thomas Cruikshanks, Lawrence; 40 years old; operative; enlisted Aug. 28, 1862.

Priv. Isaac S. Davis, Lawrence; 41 years old; teamster; enlisted Aug. 30, 1862.

Priv. Firth Dawson, Lawrence; 21 years old; operative; enlisted Sept. 1, 1862.

Priv. Patrick Dinneen, Lawrence; 19 years old; operative; enlisted Sept. 2, 1862.

Priv. Michael Dorcey, Lawrence; 22 years old; operative; enlisted Sept. 2, 1862.

Priv. Alexander Durgin, Lawrence; 41 years old; wool sorter; enlisted Aug. 30, 1862. Died May 21, 1863, of disease at New Orleans, La.

Priv. Hezekiah Eldridge, Lawrence; 19 years old; operative; enlisted Sept. 12, 1862. Deserted Nov. 25, 1862, arrested and rejoined his company March 28, 1863.

Priv. Joseph Ferren, Lawrence; 25 years old; dyer; enlisted Sept. 12, 1862. Died Aug. 16, 1863, of disease at Baton Rouge, La.

Priv. John Fitzgerald, Lawrence; 39 years old; laborer; enlisted Sept. 2, 1862. Wounded June 14, 1863, at Port Hudson, La.

Priv. John Flynn, Lawrence; 40 years old; laborer; enlisted Aug. 29, 1862. Taken prisoner June 23, 1863, at Brashear City, La.

Priv. Thomas Flynn, Lawrence; 18 years old; operative; enlisted Sept. 3, 1862.

Priv. George Fremmer, Lawrence; 21 years old; shoemaker; enlisted Sept. 9, 1862.

Priv. Jacob Fremmer, Lawrence; 29 years old; shoemaker; enlisted Sept. 9, 1862.

Priv. Asa C. Gordon, Methuen; 23 years old; farmer; enlisted Sept. 15, 1862. Wounded July 6, 1863, at Port Hudson, La.

Priv. Charles E. Greenlaw, Methuen; 21 years old; painter; enlisted Sept. 15, 1862. Wounded June 14, 1863, at Port Hudson, La.

Priv. Daniel Hart, Lawrence; 22 years old; bootmaker; enlisted Aug. 28, 1862.

Priv. Robert S. Hayes, Lawrence; 32 years old; dyer; enlisted Sept. 30, 1862.

Priv. William V. Henderson, Lawrence; 22 years old; operative; enlisted Aug. 30, 1862. Taken prisoner June 23, 1863, at Port Hudson, La.

Priv. Seth C. Hildreth, Lawrence; 18 years old; operative; enlisted Sept. 15, 1862.

Priv. William Holland, Lawrence; 35 years old; spinner; enlisted Aug. 29, 1862.

Priv. Peter Kerr, Lawrence; 31 years old; painter; enlisted Sept. 3, 1862.

Priv. Jesse P. Lane, Lawrence; 25 years old; carriage maker; enlisted Aug. 30, 1862. Taken prisoner June 23, 1863, at Brashear City, La.

Priv. James Lever, Lawrence; 32 years old; spinner; enlisted Sept. 30, 1862.

Priv. Michael Madden, Lawrence; 23 years old; seaman; enlisted Oct. 1, 1862.

Priv. Isaac Mathers, Lawrence; 43 years old; finisher; enlisted Aug. 28, 1862.

Priv. James S. McClary, Methuen; 30 years old; farmer; enlisted Sept. 15, 1862.

Priv. Lawrence McGovern, Lawrence; 18 years old; operative; enlisted Aug. 30, 1862.

Priv. John McKering, Lawrence; 35 years old; laborer; enlisted Sept. 30, 1862.

Priv. James McLellan, Lawrence; 25 years old; spinner; enlisted Sept. 3, 1862. Wounded June 14, 1863, at Port Hudson, La.

Priv. Joseph Meadowcroft, Lawrence; 18 years old; calico printer; enlisted Aug. 30, 1862.

Priv. Zachariah Morgan, Lawrence; 45 years old; bootmaker; enlisted Sept. 5, 1862.

Priv. John Morton, Lawrence; 18 years old; mechanic; enlisted Sept. 16, 1862.

Priv. George C. Mudgett, Lawrence; 32 years old; teamster; enlisted Sept. 24, 1862.

Priv. Timothy Murphy, Lawrence; 24 years old; operative; enlisted Sept. 3, 1862. Deserted Sept. 29, 1862, from Wenham, Mass.

Priv. James Nicholas, Lawrence; 25 years old; laborer; enlisted Oct. 1, 1862. Wounded June 14, 1863, at Port Hudson, La.

Priv. Charles O'Neil, Lawrence; 23 years old; spinner; enlisted Sept. 30, 1862. Discharged Feb. 25, 1863, due to disability.

Priv. Elbridge B. Osgood, Lawrence; 26 years old; clerk; enlisted Aug. 30, 1862. Transferred Dec. 11, 1862, to Company E, 48th Mass. Infantry.

Priv. James Partington, Lawrence; 19 years old; mechanic; enlisted Aug. 30, 1862.

Priv. Daniel Quinn, Lawrence; 18 years old; operative; enlisted Aug. 29, 1862. Taken prisoner June 23, 1863, at Brashear City, La.

Priv. John A. Richards, Lawrence; 21 years old; painter; enlisted Sept. 5, 1862.

Priv. Samuel Rostron, Lawrence; 35 years old; card grinder, enlisted Aug. 28, 1862.

Priv. Allen Rutherford, Lawrence; 40 years old; operative; enlisted Sept. 2, 1862. Wounded June 14, 1863, at Port Hudson, La.

Priv. Henry Scott, Lawrence; 38 years old; hostler; enlisted Sept. 5, 1862.

Priv. William Shackford, Lawrence; 28 years old; operative; enlisted Aug. 29, 1862. Taken prisoner June 23, 1863, at Brashear City, La.

Priv. William Slavin, Lawrence; 26 years old; painter; enlisted Sept. 12, 1862.

Priv. Henry N. Snell, Lawrence; 20 years old; farmer; enlisted Sept. 12, 1862. Taken prisoner June 23, 1863, at Brashear City, La.

Priv. Smardus F. Snell, Lawrence; 24 years old; clerk; enlisted Sept. 1, 1862. Taken prisoner June 23, 1863, at Brashear City, La.

Priv. George Steele, Lawrence; 24 years old; operative; enlisted Sept. 23, 1862.

Priv. Sumner Thompson, Lawrence; 31 years old; card maker; enlisted Aug. 30, 1862. Taken prisoner June 23, 1863, at Brashear City, La.

Priv. Austin B. Tobey, Lawrence; 24 years old; clerk; enlisted Aug. 30, 1862. Taken prisoner June 23, 1863, at Brashear City, La.

Priv. John W. Towle, Lawrence; 18 years old; operative; enlisted Sept. 12, 1862.

Priv. Frederick G. Trees, Lawrence; 21 years old; dyer; enlisted Sept. 1, 1862.

Priv. Henry A. Webster, Lawrence; 21 years old; operative; enlisted Sept. 1, 1862. Taken prisoner June 23, 1863, at Brashear City, La.

Priv. Frank Wermers, Lawrence; 37 years old; butcher; enlisted Aug. 28, 1862.

Priv. Elisha M. White, Charlestown; 21 years old; hospital steward; enlisted Oct. 1, 1862. Transferred Dec. 11, 1862, to 48th Mass. Infantry.

Priv. Joseph L. Whitten, Lawrence; 25 years old; wool sorter; enlisted Aug. 30, 1862. Died Aug. 10, 1863, at Baton Rouge, La.

Priv. Joseph B. Wilde, Lawrence; 45 years old; spinner; enlisted Aug. 29, 1862. Taken prisoner June 23, 1863, at Brashear City, La.

Priv. Thomas A. Wing, Lawrence; 21 years old; clerk; enlisted Aug. 29, 1862. Died of disease June 2, 1863, at Brashear City, La.

Priv. Clinton M. Wright, Lawrence; 24 years old; butcher; enlisted Aug. 29, 1862.

Priv. William G. Wright, Lawrence; 30 years old; dyer; enlisted Oct. 1, 1862. Deserted Nov. 20, 1862, from Wenham, Mass.

COMPANY I

Captain Henry B. Maglathlin, Duxbury; 44 years old; boot agent; commissioned Sept. 18, 1862. Author of a small book, *Fourth Mass. Regiment, Nine Months Volunteers, in Service, 1862–63, Company I.* It includes a very short narrative of the Louisiana campaign, but includes an extensive roster of the entire company from which most of the following individual information was derived. Captain Maglathlin was very active in education and politics and headed the enlistment drive in Duxbury in August 1862. Married and the father of 3 children, the last was born only 3 months before he was commissioned.

1st Lieut. Horatio C. Sampson, Pembroke; 31 years old; shoemaker; commissioned Sept. 18, 1862. Wounded June 14, 1863, at Port Hudson, La. Married and the father of 3 children.

2d Lieut. William F. Holmes, Kingston; 22 years old; teacher; commissioned Sept. 18, 1862. Died of disease June 3, 1863, at Brashear City, La. He was single and the first man to enlist in Kingston, Mass., for the 9-month call for volunteers.

1st Sergt. George M. Lovering, East Randolph; 32 years old; bootmaker; enlisted Sept. 22, 1862. Also served in Company D, 4th Mass. Infantry for 3-month duty in 1861. Medal of Honor winner for action June 14, 1863, at Port Hudson, La. The citation read: "During a momentary confusion in the ranks caused by other troops rushing upon the regiment, this soldier, with coolness and determination, rendered efficient aid in preventing a panic among the troops." Married and the father of 1 child. Mustered out of the 4th Mass. Infantry Aug. 28, 1863. Promoted to 1st Lieut., Oct. 19, 1863, and reported to General Andrews at Port Hudson, La., as an officer in a company of Negro troops.

Sergt. Charles N. Thayer, Pembroke; 35 years old; painter; enlisted Sept. 22, 1862. Married and the father of 1 child.

Sergt. Edwin G. Metcalf, Duxbury; 31 years old; farmer; enlisted Sept. 22, 1862. Taken prisoner June 23, 1863, at Brashear City, La. Married and the father of 1 child.

Sergt. William Kaspar, Kingston; 26 years old; baker; enlisted Sept. 22, 1862. Wounded June 14, 1863, at Port Hudson, La. Born in Bohemia. Single.

Sergt. George W. Lane, Duxbury; 29 years old; fisherman; enlisted Sept. 22, 1862. Wounded June 14, 1863, at Port Hudson, La. Married. At the time of his wounding, he was assigned to a grenade party assaulting Port Hudson. Still a private at the time, he was promoted due to his meritorious conduct.

Corpl. Thomas T. McNaught, Duxbury; 32 years old; shoemaker; enlisted Sept. 22, 1862. Married and the father of 2 children.

Corpl. Daniel Delano, Duxbury; 38 years old; carpenter; enlisted Sept. 22, 1862. Taken prisoner June 23, 1863, at Brashear City, La. Married and the father of 2 children.

Corpl. Edwin Bosworth, Pembroke; 25 years old; shoemaker; enlisted Sept. 22, 1862. Taken prisoner June 23, 1863, at Brashear City, La. Died of disease Aug. 3, 1863, at New Orleans, La. Married and the father of a 2-year-old child.

Corpl. Edward R. Church, Pembroke; 25 years old; anchor smith; enlisted Sept. 22, 1862. Married.

Corpl. Granville Baker, Duxbury; 25 years old; shoemaker; enlisted Sept. 22, 1862. Married and the father of 1 child.

Corpl. Edward F. Frost, Duxbury; 22 years old; shoemaker; enlisted Sept. 22, 1862. Taken prisoner June 23, 1863, at Brashear City, La. Single.

Corpl. Andrew Northey, Duxbury; 32 years old; mason; enlisted Sept. 22, 1862. Married and the father of 1 child.

Corpl. Jonathan F. Turner, Duxbury; 25 years old; fisherman; enlisted Sept. 22, 1862. Single.

Music Charles C. Clark, Pembroke; 19 years old; shoemaker; enlisted Sept. 22, 1862. Died of disease July 16, 1863, at New Orleans, La. Single.

Music Augustus A. Graves, Duxbury; 40 years old; peddler; enlisted Sept. 22, 1862. Married and the father of 5 children.

Wagoner John W. Brewster, Duxbury; 31 years old; shoemaker; enlisted Sept. 22, 1862. Regimental wagon master at Port Hudson. Married.

Priv. Charles E. Alden, Duxbury; 20 years old; fisherman; enlisted Sept. 22, 1862. Died of disease March 9, 1863, at Quarantine Hospital, Mississippi River, La. Single. Consent of parent given for his enlistment.

Priv. George H. Bailey, Duxbury; 33 years old; carpenter; enlisted Sept. 22, 1862. Married and the father of 2 children.

Priv. Walter Baker, Duxbury; 23 years old; shoemaker; enlisted Sept. 22, 1862. Taken prisoner June 23, 1863, at Brashear City, La. Married and the father of 2 children.

Priv. William J. Barrows, Pembroke; 23 years old; shoemaker; enlisted Sept. 22, 1862. Single.

Priv. Henry Barstow, Duxbury; 28 years old; shoecutter; enlisted Sept. 22, 1862. Taken prisoner June 23, 1863, at Brashear City, La. Single.

Priv. Joshua T. Brewster, Duxbury; 39 years old; farmer; enlisted Sept. 22, 1862. Died of disease Aug. 4, 1863, at Marine Hospital, New Orleans, La. Married and the father of 3-year-old twins.

Priv. Melzar Brewster, Jr., Duxbury; 41 years old; teamster; enlisted Sept. 22, 1862. Brother of Wagoner John Brewster. Married and father of 4 children.

Priv. Andrew C. Brigham, Hanson; 25 years old; tack maker; enlisted Sept. 22, 1862. Married and father of 1 child.

Priv. Asa Chandler, Duxbury; 29 years old; shoemaker; enlisted Sept. 22, 1862. Married and father of 2 children.

Priv. Edgar Chandler, Duxbury; 19 years old; painter; enlisted Sept. 22, 1862. Single.

Priv. Emmons A. Chandler, Duxbury; 33 years old; shoemaker; enlisted Sept. 22, 1862. Taken prisoner June 23, 1863, at Brashear City, La. Married and the father of 1 child.

Priv. Hiram Chandler, Duxbury; 41 years old; shoemaker; enlisted Sept. 22, 1862. Born in Halifax. Married and father of 3 children.

Priv. Hiram O. Chandler, Duxbury; 18 years old; shoemaker; enlisted Sept. 22, 1862. Single.

Priv. Jerome Chandler, Duxbury; 35 years old; carpenter; enlisted Sept. 22, 1862. Married and the father of 1 child.

Appointed Corpl., Sept. 23, 1862, but reduced to the ranks June 22, 1863.

Priv. John A Chandler, Kingston; 28 years old; farmer; enlisted Sept. 22, 1862. Discharged due to disability Feb. 4, 1863, at Boston, Mass. Married and the father of 4 children.

Priv. Noah J. Chandler, Duxbury; 22 years old; shoemaker; enlisted Sept. 22, 1862. Taken prisoner June 23, 1863, at Brashear City, La. Brother of Asa. Single.

Priv. Philip H. Chandler, Pembroke; 23 years old; shoemaker; enlisted Sept. 22, 1862. Taken prisoner June 23, 1863, at Brashear City, La. Single.

Priv. William E. Chandler, Pembroke; 23 years old; farmer; enlisted Sept. 22, 1862. Taken prisoner June 23, 1863, at Brashear City, La. Born in Halifax. Single.

Priv. George H. Church, Pembroke; 30 years old; farmer; enlisted Sept. 22, 1862. Married and the father of 3 children.

Priv. George L. Churchill, Kingston; 21 years old; farmer; enlisted Sept. 22, 1862. Taken prisoner June 23, 1863, at Brashear City, La. Single.

Priv. Stephen Clark, Jr., Duxbury; 29 years old; farmer; enlisted Sept. 22, 1862. Died of disease July 16, 1863, at Algiers, La. Single.

Priv. Edwin B. Cook, Hanson; 24 years old; tackmaker; enlisted Sept. 22, 1862. Taken prisoner June 23, 1863, at Brashear City, La. Single.

Priv. Robert H. Cornell, Pembroke; 21 years old; farmer; enlisted Sept. 22, 1862. Died of disease April 22, 1863, at New Orleans, La. Single.

Priv. James B. Curtis, Pembroke; 46 years old; carpenter; enlisted Sept. 22, 1862. Died of disease April 29, 1863, at New Orleans, La. Married and the father of 4 children.

Priv. Augustine A. Delano, Duxbury; 19 years old; farmer; enlisted Sept. 22, 1862. Taken prisoner June 23, 1863, at Brashear City, La. Single.

Priv. Daniel W. Delano, Duxbury; 22 years old; fisherman; enlisted Sept. 22, 1862. Died of disease March 22, 1863, at New Orleans, La. Single.

Priv. Hiram T. Delano, Duxbury; 20 years old; fisherman; enlisted Sept. 22, 1862. Taken prisoner June 23, 1863, at Brashear City, La. Brother of Augustine. Single.

Priv. Oscar Delano, Duxbury; 22 years old; harness maker; enlisted Sept. 22, 1862. Died of diphtheria Aug. 15, 1863, at Indianapolis, Ind. Single.

Priv. George H. Ford, Pembroke; 21 years old; shoemaker; enlisted Sept. 22, 1862. Died of disease July 17, 1863, at New Orleans, La. Single.

Priv. Joseph P. Ford, Pembroke; 20 years old; shoemaker; enlisted Sept. 22, 1862. Single.

Priv. Walter H. Freeman, Duxbury; 21 years old; farmer; enlisted Sept. 22, 1862. Single.

Priv. Harrison T. Glass, Duxbury; 23 years old; farmer; enlisted Sept. 22, 1862. Taken prisoner June 23, 1863, at Brashear City, La. Died of disease July 30, 1863, at Port Hudson, La. Single.

Priv. George A. Graves, Duxbury; 18 years old; farmer; enlisted Sept. 22, 1862. Single. In target-shooting competition in Baton Rouge, proved to be the best shot in the regiment.

Priv. Benjamin F. Gray, Kingston; 19 years old; farmer; enlisted Sept. 22, 1862. Married.

Priv. Bailey Gullefer, Duxbury; 32 years old; caulker; enlisted Sept. 22, 1862. Taken prisoner June 23, 1863, at Brashear City, La. Married and the father of 1 child.

Priv. Elihu Harriman, Duxbury; 25 years old; shoemaker; enlisted Sept. 22, 1862. Taken prisoner June 23, 1863, at Brashear City, La. Married and the father of 1 child.

Priv. George L. Higgins, Duxbury; 44 years old; carpenter; enlisted Sept. 22, 1862. Married and the father of 4 children.

Priv. Allyn Holmes, Jr., Kingston; 21 years old; teacher; enlisted Sept. 22, 1862. Died of disease March 28, 1863, at Baton Rouge, La. Single.

Priv. Henry S. Holmes, Kingston; 20 years old; laborer; enlisted Sept. 22, 1862. Single.

Priv. Alden Howard, Pembroke; 40 years old; teamster; enlisted Sept. 22, 1862. Died of disease July 16, 1863, at New Orleans, La. Single.

Priv. Nathan Howard, Pembroke; 31 years old; farmer; enlisted Sept. 22, 1862. Taken prisoner June 23, 1863, at Brashear City, La. Married and the father of 2 children.

Priv. Wadsworth Hunt, Duxbury; 45 years old; mariner; enlisted Sept. 22, 1862. Married and the father of 4 children.

Priv. Willliam F. Hunt, Duxbury; 36 years old; fisherman; enlisted Sept. 22, 1862. Taken prisoner June 23, 1863, at Brashear City, La. Brother of Wadsworth. Married and the father of 4 children.

Priv. John Jones, Pembroke; 28 years old; engineer; enlisted Sept. 22, 1862. Died of measles June 11, 1863, at Brashear City, La. Married and the father of 1 child.

Priv. William W. Jones, Duxbury; 28 years old; mariner; enlisted Sept. 22, 1862. Married and the father of 1 child. Member of the Pioneer Corps in the Teche and second Port Hudson expeditions.

Priv. Abel W. Keene, Pembroke; 20 years old; farmer; enlisted Sept. 22, 1862. Single.

Priv. Nathan C. Keene, Pembroke; 33 years old; caulker; enlisted Sept. 22, 1862. Taken prisoner June 23, 1863, at Brashear City, La. Married and the father of 3 children.

Priv. Albert Lapham, Pembroke; 22 years old; shoemaker; enlisted Sept. 22, 1862. Single.

Priv. Luther T. Lapham, Pembroke; 18 years old; shoemaker; enlisted Sept. 22, 1862. Taken prisoner June 23, 1863, at Brashear City, La. Single.

Priv. Bernard Loring, Pembroke; 31 years old; shoemaker; enlisted Sept. 22, 1862. Married, father of 2 children.

Priv. Morton M. Loring, Pembroke; 20 years old; carpenter; enlisted Sept. 22, 1862. Taken prisoner June 23, 1863, at Brashear City, La. Single.

Priv. Elisha S. Lucas, Westboro; 24 years old; farmer; enlisted Sept. 22, 1862. Single. Appointed Corpl., Sept. 23, 1862; reduced to ranks March 21, 1863.

Priv. Jerry McCarty, Kingston; 22 years old; farmer; enlisted Sept. 22, 1862. Born in Cork, Ireland. Single.

Priv. Nahum McFarlin, Pembroke; 22 years old; shoemaker; enlisted Sept. 22, 1862. Married and the father of 1 child.

Priv. Thomas M. Nash, Pembroke; 19 years old; farmer; enlisted Sept. 22, 1862. Single.

Priv. William F. Nash, Pembroke; 30 years old; shoemaker; enlisted Sept. 22, 1862. Married and the father of 4 children.

Priv. Adoniram J. Oldham, Kingston; 27 years old; mason; enlisted Sept. 22, 1862. Single.

Priv. Samuel A. Page, Pembroke; 19 years old; painter; enlisted Sept. 22, 1862. Single.

Priv. Calvin Peterson, Pembroke; 36 years old; box maker; enlisted Sept. 22, 1862. Taken prisoner June 23, 1863, at Brashear City, La. Married.

Priv. Waldo H. Peterson, Kingston; 19 years old; rigger; enlisted Sept. 22, 1862. Wounded June 14, 1863, at Port Hudson, La. Died Sept. 5, 1863. Single.

Priv. Walter Peterson, Duxbury; 20 years old; farmer; enlisted Sept. 22, 1862. Died of typhoid fever Aug. 3, 1863, at Port Hudson, La. Single.

Priv. Thomas Prince, Kingston; 22 years old; tobacconist; enlisted Sept. 22, 1862. Single.

Priv. Francis J. Randall, Duxbury; 25 years old; horse dealer; enlisted Sept. 22, 1862. Single.

Priv. Marcus M. Reed, Pembroke; 27 years old; shoemaker; enlisted Sept. 22, 1862. Died of disease June 8, 1863, at Brashear City, La. Single.

Priv. George F. Ryder, Duxbury; 26 years old; shoemaker; enlisted Sept. 22, 1862. Maglathlin does not include this man in his roster.

Priv. Azor H. Sampson, Pembroke; 30 years old; painter; enlisted Sept. 22, 1862. Taken prisoner June 23, 1863, at Brashear City, La. Married and the father of 2 children.

Priv. George B. Sampson, Duxbury; 36 years old; shoemaker; enlisted Sept. 22, 1862. Died of disease July 11, 1863, at New Orleans, La. Married and the father of 7 children.

Priv. George B. Simmons, Duxbury; 21 years old; shoemaker; enlisted Sept. 22, 1862. Single.

Priv. John W. Stetson, Pembroke; 19 years old; shoemaker; enlisted Sept. 22, 1862. Single.

Priv. Edward D. Swift, Duxbury; 19 years old; farmer; enlisted Sept. 22, 1862. Single.

Priv. William T. Swift, Duxbury; 20 years old; farmer; enlisted Sept. 22, 1862. Taken prisoner June 23, 1863, at Brashear City, La. Brother of Edward. Married.

Priv. Albert M. Thayer, Hanson; 28 years old; tack maker; enlisted Sept. 22, 1862. Married and the father of 2 children. Brother of Charles, a Sergt. in Company I.

Priv. John P. Tillson, Pembroke; 23 years old; shoemaker; enlisted Sept. 22, 1862. Taken prisoner June 23, 1863, at Brashear City, La. Single.

Priv. George H. Torrey, Duxbury; 31 years old; fisherman; enlisted Sept. 22, 1862. Single.

Priv. William Wadsworth, Duxbury; 24 years old; mariner; enlisted Sept. 22, 1862. Wounded June 14, 1863, at Port Hudson, La. Died from battle wounds July 24, 1863, at Baton Rouge, La. Single.

Priv. Nathaniel A. Washburn, Kingston; 21 years old; farmer; enlisted Sept. 22, 1862. Taken prisoner June 23, 1863, at Brashear City, La. Died of diphtheria Aug. 8, 1863, aboard the steamer *North America*, on the Mississippi River. Buried at Helena, Ark. Single.

Priv. Augustus Weston, Duxbury; 35 years old; farmer; enlisted Sept. 22, 1862. Taken prisoner June 23, 1863, at Brashear City, La. Appointed Sergt. Dec. 6, 1862, and reduced to the ranks July 31, 1863. Married and the father of 3 children.

Priv. George S. Weston, Duxbury; 22 years old; fisherman; enlisted Sept. 22, 1862. Single.

Priv. James H. Weston, Duxbury; 34 years old; farmer; enlisted Sept. 22, 1862. Died of disease May 1, 1863, at New Orleans, La. Married and the father of 2 children.

Priv. George M. Witherell, Pembroke; 36 years old; box maker; enlisted Sept. 22, 1862. Died of disease March 28, 1863, at Baton Rouge, La. Married and the father of 1 child.

Priv. Martin S. Witherell, Pembroke; 41 years old; box maker; enlisted Sept. 22, 1862. Brother of George. Married and the father of 2 children.

Company K

Captain William H. Bartlett, Taunton; 38 years old; manufacturer; commissioned Aug. 29, 1862. Killed June 14, 1863, at Port Hudson, La. Also served in Company G, 4th Mass. Infantry for 3-month duty in 1861.

1st Lieut. John H. Church, Taunton; 25 years old; clerk; commissioned Aug. 29. 1862. Wounded June 14, 1863, at Port Hudson, La. Also served in Company G, 4th Mass. Infantry for 3-month duty in 1861.

2d Lieut. Philander Williams, Taunton; 33 years old; grocer; commissioned Aug. 29, 1862. Acting regimental quartermaster April 3–Aug. 1, 1863.

1st Sergt. Simeon G. Blandin, Taunton; 41 years old; sawyer; enlisted Sept. 15, 1862. Taken prisoner June 23, 1863, at Brashear City, La. Also served in Company F, 4th Mass. Infantry for 3-month duty in 1861.

Sergt. Caleb C. Collins, Taunton; 31 years old; machinist; enlisted Sept. 15, 1862.

Sergt. Michael Murphy, Taunton; 25 years old; soldier; enlisted Sept. 15, 1862. Detailed as Color Sergt., Dec. 22, 1862.

Sergt. William W. Smith, Berkley; 23 years old; painter; enlisted Sept. 15, 1862. Also served in Company G, 4th Mass. Infantry for 3-month duty in 1861.

Sergt. Samuel H. Morse, Taunton; 26 years old; clerk; enlisted Sept. 15, 1862.

Sergt. George E. Payson, Taunton; 28 years old; printer; enlisted Sept. 15, 1862. Died of disease April 4, 1863, at Baton Rouge, La.

Corpl. Edgar R. Sprague, Taunton; 23 years old; machinist; enlisted Sept. 15, 1862. Taken prisoner June 23, 1863, at Brashear City, La.

Corpl. James H. Leach, Easton; 30 years old; bootmaker; enlisted Sept. 23, 1862.

Corpl. William R. Morris, Taunton; 32 years old; fireman; enlisted Sept. 15, 1862.

Corpl. Stephen Sweetser, Taunton; 25 years old; supervisor; enlisted Sept. 15, 1862.

Corpl. Tilson Fuller, Taunton; 30 years old; clerk; enlisted Sept. 15, 1862.

Corpl. Ebenezer Bowman, Taunton; 31 years old; manufacturer; enlisted Sept. 15, 1862. Taken prisoner June 23, 1863, at Brashear City, La.

Corpl. William Dean, Jr., Taunton; 34 years old; shoemaker; enlisted Sept. 15, 1862.

Corpl. Nathan A. Simmons, Taunton; 31 years old; occupation not given; enlisted Sept. 15, 1862. Deserted Jan. 8, 1863, from a hospital in New York City.

Music James A. Bracken, Taunton; 20 years old; brittannia worker; enlisted Sept. 15, 1862.

Music Allen K. Bassett, Taunton; 14 years old; student; enlisted Sept. 15, 1862. Taken prisoner June 23, 1863, at Brashear City, La.

Wagoner Manning W. Fox, Taunton; 39 years old; burnisher; enlisted Sept. 15, 1862. Taken prisoner June 23, 1863, at Brashear City, La.

Priv. Joseph A. Alden, Wareham; 27 years old; nailer; enlisted Sept. 15, 1862.

Priv. Haynes C. Aldrich, Taunton; 23 years old; cooper; enlisted Sept. 15, 1862.

Priv. Zephaniah G. P. Andrews, Taunton; 32 years old; laborer; enlisted Sept. 15, 1862. Died of disease May 7, 1863, at New Orleans, La.

Priv. David Babbitt, Taunton; 30 years old; core maker; enlisted Sept. 15, 1862. Taken prisoner June 23, 1863, at Brashear City, La.

Priv. Charles H. Barrows, Taunton; 20 years old; spinner; enlisted Sept. 15, 1862.

Priv. Orin L. Bassett, Taunton; 38 years old; nailer; enlisted Sept. 15, 1862.

Priv. Nelson Billington, Taunton; 35 years old; packer; enlisted Sept. 15, 1862.

Priv. Reinhold Bubser, Taunton; 29 years old; moulder; enlisted Sept. 15, 1862.

Priv. Daniel W. Burrell, Easton; 30 years old; shoemaker; enlisted Sept. 23, 1862.

Priv. Charles H. Burt, Taunton; 20 years old; laborer; enlisted Sept. 15, 1862.

Priv. Alexander R. Cain, Raynham; 18 years old; shoemaker; enlisted Sept. 15, 1862.

Priv. John Carr, Edgartown, 26 years old; machinist; enlisted Sept. 15, 1862. Killed June 14, 1863, at Port Hudson, La.

Priv. William Carr, Taunton; 45 years old; laborer; enlisted Sept. 15, 1862.

Priv. John Cassidy, Taunton; 35 years old; laborer; enlisted Sept. 15, 1862. Died of disease July 18, 1863, at Port Hudson, La.

Priv. Charles H. Caswell, Taunton; 18 years old; hostler; enlisted Sept. 15, 1862.

Priv. Otis Caswell, Taunton; 33 years old; laborer; enlisted Sept. 15, 1862. Taken prisoner June 23, 1863, at Brashear City, La.

Priv. Ezekiel W. Chamberlain, Taunton; 27 years old; carpenter; enlisted Sept. 15, 1862.

Priv. Alvin R. Dean, Taunton; 18 years old; laborer; enlisted Sept. 15, 1862. Wounded June 14, 1863, at Port Hudson, La. Died from wounds July 22, 1863, at Baton Rouge, La.

Priv. Charles E. Dean, Taunton; 21 years old; moulder; enlisted Sept. 15, 1862.

Priv. George E. Dean, Taunton; 22 years old; clerk; enlisted Sept. 15, 1862. Wounded June 14, 1863, at Port Hudson, La.

Priv. Alexander Drape, Taunton; 30 years old; teamer; enlisted Sept. 15, 1862.

Priv. William M. Eddy, Taunton; 44 years old; teamer; enlisted Sept. 15, 1862. Died Aug. 8, 1863, on board a steamer on the Mississippi River.

Priv. Reuben Ellis, Taunton; 43 years old; occupation not given; enlisted Sept. 15, 1862. Discharged Nov. 21, 1862, at Boston, Mass.

Priv. George W. Field, Taunton; 19 years old; farmer; enlisted Sept. 15, 1862.

Priv. Lewis B. Field, Taunton; 21 years old; laborer; enlisted Sept. 15, 1862.

Priv. George S. Fox, Acushnet; 18 years old; clerk; enlisted Sept. 15, 1862. Wounded June 14, 1863, at Port Hudson, La.

Priv. William A. French, Berkley; 18 years old; farmer; enlisted Sept. 15, 1862.

Priv. Michael Gaffney, Taunton; 32 years old; laborer; enlisted Sept. 15, 1862.

Priv. James Galligan, Taunton; 18 years old; laborer; enlisted Sept. 15, 1862. Wounded and taken prisoner June 14, 1863, at Port Hudson, La.

Priv. Thomas Gibbons, Jr., Taunton; 18 years old; sailor; enlisted Sept. 15, 1862.

Priv. William J. Gilbert, Taunton; 36 years old; harness maker; enlisted Sept. 15, 1862.

Priv. Oliver C. Gurney, Taunton; 19 years old; moulder; enlisted Sept. 15, 1862.

Priv. Francis R. Hall, Raynham; 19 years old; farmer; enlisted Sept. 15, 1862. Killed June 14, 1863, at Port Hudson, La.

Priv. Charles H. Hamilton, Taunton; 19 years old; painter; enlisted Sept. 15, 1862.

Priv. George H. Handy, Taunton; 19 years old; laborer; enlisted Sept. 15, 1862.

Priv. James B. Hathaway, Taunton; 18 years old; nailer; enlisted Sept. 15, 1862. Taken prisoner June 23, 1863, at Brashear City, La.

Priv. Charles H. Hewitt, Taunton; 18 years old; farmer; enlisted Sept. 15, 1862. Wounded June 14, 1863, at Port Hudson, La.

Priv. David Howard, Easton; 34 years old; shoemaker; enlisted Sept. 23, 1862.

Priv. Leprelate King, New Bedford; 39 years old; grocer; enlisted Sept. 15, 1862. Died of disease June 11, 1863, at Brashear City, La.

Priv. Thomas Larkin, Taunton; 19 years old; teamer; enlisted Nov. 3, 1862. Taken prisoner June 23, 1863, at Brashear City, La.

Priv. John Malloy, Taunton; 39 years old; laborer; enlisted Sept. 15, 1862.

Priv. Michael Milrick, Easton; 19 years old; shoemaker; enlisted Sept. 23, 1862. Died of disease June 21, 1863, at Brashear City, La.

Priv. Edgar L. Morse, Taunton; 20 years old; farmer; enlisted Sept. 15, 1862. Wounded June 14, 1863, at Port Hudson, La.

Priv. Daniel Murphy, Easton; 19 years old; shoemaker; enlisted Sept. 23, 1862.

Priv. Ephraim F. Norcutt, Berkley; 18 years old; coaster; enlisted Sept. 15, 1862. Taken prisoner June 23, 1863, at Brashear City, La. Died of disease Aug. 17, 1863, in Rochester, N.Y.

Priv. Gilbert M. O'Neill, Taunton; 18 years old; merchant; enlisted Sept. 15, 1862. Wounded June 14, 1863, at Port Hudson, La.

Priv. Enoch J. O'Shea, Easton; 32 years old; grocer; enlisted Sept. 23, 1862. Taken prisoner June 23, 1863, at Brashear City, La.

Priv. George E. Packard, Easton; 18 years old; farmer; enlisted Sept. 23, 1862.

Priv. William M. Packard, Easton; 22 years old; farmer; enlisted Sept. 23, 1862. Died of disease July 12, 1863, at Baton Rouge, La.

Priv. Peter W. Packer, Taunton; 44 years old; machinist; enlisted Sept. 23, 1862.

Priv. Edwin Park, Taunton; 45 years old; paper maker; enlisted Sept. 15, 1862.

Priv. Benjamin F. Paull, Taunton; 36 years old; farmer; enlisted Sept. 15, 1862. Died of disease Aug. 27, 1863, at Taunton, Mass.

Priv. Henry C. Porter, Taunton; 42 years old; clerk; enlisted Sept. 15, 1862. Taken prisoner June 23, 1863, at Brashear City, La.

Priv. Albert S. Pratt, Dighton; 21 years old; farmer; enlisted Sept. 15, 1862.

Priv. Daniel Quane, Easton; 19 years old; shoemaker; enlisted Sept. 23, 1862.

Priv. William Quillan, Taunton; 20 years old; painter; enlisted Sept. 15, 1862.

Priv. John R. Reed, Taunton; 37 years old; farmer; enlisted Sept. 15, 1862. Died Sept. 14, 1863, at a hospital in Rochester, N.Y.

Priv. John Reynolds, Taunton; 32 years old; laborer; enlisted Sept. 15, 1862. Taken prisoner June 23, 1863, at Brashear City, La.

Priv. John Rigney, Easton; 34 years old; farmer; enlisted Sept. 23, 1862.

Priv. Edward P. Roach, Taunton; 18 years old; nailer; enlisted Sept. 15, 1862.

Priv. William H. Rothwell, Taunton; 45 years old; machinist; enlisted Sept. 15, 1862.

Priv. Hanson L. Smart, Taunton; 45 years old; carpenter; enlisted Sept. 15, 1862. Died Aug. 4, 1863, in camp at Port Hudson, La.

Priv. George W. Standish, Taunton; 30 years old; machinist; enlisted Sept. 15, 1862. Wounded June 14, 1863, at Port Hudson, La. Died of wounds June 29, 1863, at New Orleans, La.

Priv. Charles E. Strange, Taunton; 23 years old; laborer; enlisted Sept. 15, 1862.

Priv. Henry E. Strout, Easton; 22 years old; brakeman; enlisted Sept. 23, 1862. Wounded June 14, 1863, at Port Hudson, La.

Priv. George A. Tilden, Easton; 18 years old; shovel maker; enlisted Sept. 15, 1862. Missing June 14, 1863, at Port Hudson, La. Died of disease July 30, 1863, in camp at Port Hudson, La.

Priv. William E. Tisdale, Taunton; 30 years old; painter; enlisted Sept. 23, 1862.

Priv. Edwin R. Townsend, Taunton; 31 years old; dentist; enlisted Sept. 15, 1862.

Priv. Joseph F. Tripp, Taunton; 27 years old; painter; enlisted Sept. 15, 1862. Taken prisoner June 23, 1863, at Brashear City, La.

Priv. Patrick Ward, Taunton; 18 years old; laborer; enlisted Sept. 15, 1862.

Priv. David Whalen, Easton; 29 years old; laborer; enlisted Sept. 23, 1862.

Priv. Alden Whitman, Raynham; 31 years old; shoemaker; enlisted Sept. 15, 1862. Taken prisoner June 23, 1863, at Brashear City, La.

Priv. Sylvester S. Whitman, Raynham; 35 years old; shoemaker; enlisted Sept. 15, 1862. Taken prisoner June 23, 1863, at Brashear City, La.

Priv. William E. Wilcox, Taunton; 22 years old; nailer; enlisted Sept. 15, 1862.

Priv. Alfred M. Williams, Taunton; 21 years old; farmer; enlisted Sept. 15, 1862.

Priv. John Williams, Dighton; 29 years old; painter; enlisted Dec. 8, 1862. Deserted Dec. 9, 1862, at Taunton, Mass.

Priv. William Wood, Taunton; 39 years old; machinist; enlisted Sept. 15, 1862.

Priv. William C. Wood, Taunton; 26 years old; machinist; enlisted Sept. 15, 1862.

Priv. John G. Wright, Taunton; 22 years old; agent; enlisted Sept. 15, 1862.

Priv. John E. Young, Taunton; 28 years old; moulder; enlisted Sept. 15, 1862.

Notes

Chapter I

1. Patricia L. Faust, ed., *Historical Times Illustrated Encyclopedia of the Civil War* (New York: Harper and Row, 1986), 564.
2. E. B. Long and Barbara Long, *The Civil War Day by Day* (New York: DaCapa Press, 1971), 726. The figures shown in the text are not adjusted to today's dollar value but reflect actual worth during the middle 1800s.
3. Geoffrey C. Ward, and Ric and Ken Burns, contributors, *The Civil War: An Illustrated History* (New York: Alfred A. Knoff, 1990), 108.
4. Massachusetts AGO, *Massachusetts Soldiers, Sailors and Marines in the Great Civil War* (Norwood, Mass.: Norwood Printing, 1931), 1–68. Troop strength for each company was computed using the regimental roster.
5. *Revised Regulations for the Army of the United States, 1861* (1861; reprint, Harrisburg, Pa.: National Historical Society, 1990), 21–24, 476–82.
6. Warren K. Tice, *Uniform Buttons of the United States, 1776–1865* (Gettysburg, Pa.: Thomas Publications, 1997), 328.
7. James F. Dargan, *My Experiences in Service or, A Nine-Months Man* (1873; Los Angeles: California State University, 1974), book 1 entries, 9/30/62, 10/11/62, 10/13/62, and 10/16/62.

Chapter II

1. Ezra J. Warner, *Generals in Blue* (Baton Rouge: Louisiana State University Press, 1964), 17–18.
2. Ibid., 60–61.
3. Faust, 320.
4. Ibid., 254.
5. Ezra J. Warner, *Generals in Gray* (Baton Rouge: Louisiana State University Press, 1959), 161–62.
6. Jim Miles, *A River Unvexed* (Nashville, Tenn.: Rutledge Hill Press, 1994), 252–54.
7. Faust, 242.

Chapter III

1. Warner, *Generals in Gray,* 97.
2. Warner, *Generals in Blue,* 9.
3. Ibid., 134–35.
4. Faust, 243.
5. *War of the Rebellion: A Compilation of the Official Records of the Union and Confederate Armies,* ser. 1, vol. 26 (Washington, D.C.: Government Printing Office, 1891), 530. Hereinafter cited as OR.
6. Dargan, book 2, entry 2/16/63.
7. Ibid., book 2, entries 2/18/63, 2/20/63, 2/23/63.

Chapter IV

1. Lawrence Lee Hewitt, *Port Hudson Confederate Bastion on the Mississippi* (Baton Rouge: Louisiana State University Press, 1987), 63.
2. Edward Cunningham, *The Port Hudson Campaign, 1862–1863* (Baton Rouge: Louisiana State University Press, 1963), 19.
3. Miles, 519–22.
4. Dargan, book 2, entry 3/16/63; book 3, entry 3/17/63.
5. Dargan, book 3, entry 3/26/63.

Chapter V

1. Dargan, book 3, entry 4/2/63.
2. Warner, *Generals in Gray,* 299–300.
3. Ibid., 276–77.
4. T. Michael Parrish, *Richard Taylor Soldier Prince of Dixie* (Chapel Hill: The University of North Carolina Press, 1992), 271–72.
5. Ibid., 274.
6. Dargan, book 3, entry 4/27/63.
7. *Revised Regulations for the Army of the United States, 1861,* 341–46.

Chapter VI

1. John D. Winters, *The Civil War in Louisiana* (Baton Rouge: Louisiana State University Press, 1963), 237.
2. OR, ser. 1, vol. 26, 572–73.
3. Ibid., 494.
4. Ibid., 183–85.
5. Dargan, book 3, entry 5/31/63.

Chapter VII

1. Hewitt, 127.
2. Ibid., 136. It is difficult to determine the actual number of Union troops who fought at Port Hudson on May 27, 1863. Hewitt states Banks' 30,000 Union men outnumbered the Confederates four to one. OR, ser. 1, vol. 26, 43–45, asserts the number at 13,000 men. OR, ser. 1, vol. 26, 527–28, troop strength reports, dated May 31, indicate approximately 33,000 in front of Port Hudson. Faust, 596, maintains 30,000 men were available, but Banks utilized a small segment.
3. OR, ser. 1, vol. 26, 519–20. Confederate troop figures differ. Banks' letter to Grant estimates enemy strength at 5,000 to 6,000. OR, ser. 1, vol. 26, 43–45, Banks states 8,000 men defending Port Hudson. OR, ser. 1, vol. 26, 536. Confederate deserters claim 5,000 men within the fort. Faust, 596, declares Gardner had 7,000 soldiers within the garrison.
4. OR, ser. 1, vol. 26, 126–28.
5. Ibid., 534–35.
6. Ibid., 552–53.
7. Dargan, book 4, entry 6/15/63.
8. OR, ser. 1, vol. 26, 69.
9. Ibid., 603.
10. W. F. Beyer and O. F. Keydel, eds., *Deeds of Valor* (1903; reprint, Stamford, Conn., Longmeadow Press, 1994), 552, 554.
11. OR, ser. 1, vol. 26, 911–14.

Chapter VIII

1. OR, ser. 1, vol. 26, 182.
2. Ibid., 620.
3. Ibid., 5, 17.
4. Ibid., 648.

Chapter IX

1. Dargan, book 3, entry 8/12/63.
2. Faust, 656. The Sanitary Commission was the Red Cross of the Civil War.
3. Frederick H. Dyer, *A Compedium of the War of the Rebellion* (Dayton, Ohio: Morningside, 1979), 1249.
4. Dargan, book 3, entry 8/27/63.

Bibliography

BOOKS

Battles and Leaders of the Civil War. 4 vols. Edison, N.J.: Castle Books, 1956.

Beyer, W. F., and O. F. Keydel. *Deeds of Valor.* 1903. Reprint, Stamford, Conn.: Longmeadow Press, 1994.

Bowen, James L. *Massachusetts in the War.* Springfield, Mass.: Clark W. Bryan, 1889.

Broadwater, Robert P. "The Greenbolt Action." North South Trader's Civil War Magazine, vol. 26, no. 4. Orange, Va.: 1999.

Catton, Bruce. *Grant Takes Command.* New York: Little, Brown and Co., 1969.

Chestnut, Mary. *A Diary from Dixie.* 1905. Reprint, New York: Random House, 1997.

Coombe, Jack D. *Gunfire around the Gulf.* New York: Bantam Books, 1999.

Cowles, Calvin D. *Atlas to Accompany the Official Records of the Union and Confederate Armies.* Washington, D.C.: Government Printing Office, 1895.

Cunningham, Edward. *The Port Hudson Campaign, 1862–1863.* Baton Rouge: Louisiana State University Press, 1963.

Cunningham, H. H. *Doctors in Gray.* Second edition. Baton Rouge: Louisiana State University Press, 1960.

Dargan, James F. *My Experiences in Service, or A Nine Months Man.* Special collection. Los Angeles: California State University, 1974.

Dawson, Sarah Morgan. *A Confederate Girl's Diary.* 1913. Reprint, Bloomington: Indiana University Press, 1968.

Dengler, Eartha, Katherine Khalife, and Ken Skulski. *Images of America, Lawrence, Massachusetts.* Dover, N.H.: Arcadia Publishing, 1995.

Dorgins, M. P. *History of Lawrence, Massachusetts.* Cambridge, Mass.: Murray Printing Co., 1924.

Dyer, Frederick H. *A Compendium of the War of the Rebellion.* Vol. 2. Dayton, Ohio: Morningside, 1979.

Ellsworth, Edward W. *Massachusetts in the Civil War.* Vol. 3. Boston: Massachusetts Civil War Centennial Commission, 1962.

Faust, Patricia L., ed. *Historical Times Illustrated Encyclopedia of the Civil War.* New York: Harper and Row, 1986.

Fiore, Jordan D. *Massachusetts in the Civil War.* Vol. 2. Boston: Massachusetts Civil War Centennial Commission, 1961.

Garofalo, Robert, and Mark Elrod. *Civil War Era Musical Instruments and Military Bands.* Charleston, W.Va.: Pictorial Histories Publishing Co., 1985.

Garrison, Webb. *Lincoln's Little War.* Nashville, Tenn.: Rutledge Hill Press, 1997.

Grisamore, Silas T. *The Civil War Reminiscences of Major Silas T. Grisamore.* Baton Rouge: Louisiana State University Press, 1993.

Henry, Robert Selph. *The Story of the Confederacy.* Indianapolis: Bobbs Merrill Co., 1931.

Hewitt, Lawrence Lee. *Port Hudson, Confederate Bastion on the Mississippi.* Baton Rouge: Louisiana State University Press, 1987.

Irwin, Richard B. *History of the Nineteenth Army Corps.* New York: G. P. Putman's Sons, 1893.

Lee, Fitzhugh. *General Lee.* 1894. Reprint, Wilmington, N.C.: Broadfoot Publishing Co., 1989.

Long, E. B., and Barbara Long. *The Civil War Day by Day.* New York: Da Capo Press, Inc., 1971.

Lord, Francis A., and Arthur Wise. *Bands and Drummer Boys of the Civil War.* South Brunswick, N.J.: Thomas Yoseloff, 1966.

Maglathlin, Henry B. *Company I, Fourth Massachusetts Regiment, Nine Months Volunteers in Service, 1862–63.* Boston, Mass.: George C. Rand and Avery, 1863.

Marius Richard, ed. *The Columbia Book of Civil War Poetry.* New York: Columbia University Press, 1994.

Massachusetts, Adjutant General's Office. *Massachusetts Soldiers, Sailors, and Marines in the Great Civil War.* Vol. 1. Norwood, Mass.: Norwood Printing, 1931.

McGuinn, William F., and Bruce S. Bazelon. *American Military Button Makers and Dealers: Their Backmarks and Dates.* Chelsea, Mich.: Book Crafters, Inc., 1990.

McPherson, James M. *Battle Cry of Freedom.* New York: Oxford University Press, Inc., 1988.

McPherson, James M. *For Cause and Comrades.* New York: Oxford University Press, Inc., 1997.

McPherson, James M., and Patricia R. McPherson. *Lamson of the Gettysburg.* New York: Oxford University Press, Inc., 1997.

Miles, Jim. *A River Unvexed.* Nashville, Tenn.: Rutledge Hill Press, 1994.

Oates, Stephen B. *The Whirlwind of the War: Voices of the Storm, 1861–1865.* New York: Harper Collins Publishers, Inc., 1998.

O'Connor, Thomas H. *Massachusetts in the Civil War.* Vol. 1. Boston: Massachusetts Civil War Centennial Commission, 1960.

Parrish, T. Michael. *Richard Taylor, Soldier Prince of Dixie.* Chapel Hill: The University of North Carolina Press, 1992.

Porter, Horace. *Campaigning with Grant.* New York: Mallard Press, 1991.

Revised Regulations for the Army of the United States, 1861. Reprint, Harrisburg, Pa.: National Historical Society, 1990.

Robertson, James I., Jr. *Stonewall Jackson: The Man, The Soldier, The Legend.* New York: Macmillan Publishing, 1997.

Simpson, Brooks D. *Ulysses S. Grant.* New York: Houghton Mifflin Co., 2000.

Skulski, Ken. *Images of America, Lawrence, Massachusetts.* Vol. 2. Dover, N.H.: Arcadia Publishing, 1997.

Tice, Warren K. *Uniform Buttons of the United States, 1776–1865.* Gettysburg, Pa.: Thomas Publications, 1997.

War of the Rebellion: A Compilation of the Official Records of the Union and Confederate Armies. 128 vols. Washington, D.C.: Government Printing Office, 1880–1901.

Ward, Geoffrey C., Ric Burns, and Ken Burns. *The Civil War, An Illustrated History.* New York: Alfred A. Knopf, Inc., 1990.

Warner, Ezra J. *Generals in Blue.* Baton Rouge: Louisiana State University Press, 1964.

Warner Ezra J. *Generals in Gray.* Baton Rouge: Louisiana State University Press, 1959.

Welsh, Douglas. *The Civil War, A Complete Military History.* New York: Gallery Books, 1981.

Winters, John D. *The Civil War in Louisiana.* Baton Rouge: Louisiana State University Press, 1963.

Woodworth, Steven E. *Jefferson Davis and His Generals.* Lawrence, Kans.: University Press of Kansas, 1990.

OTHER SOURCES

Immigrant City Archives, Lawrence, Mass. Local material collection.

Lawrence Public Library. Special collection. Grand Army of the Republic records and Civil War rosters.

North Andover Historical Society, North Andover, Mass. Local material collection.

United States Army Military History Institute, Carlisle, Pa. Photographic archives and personal papers.

Index